Meditation for Children

Pathways to Happiness, Harmony, Creativity & Fun for the Family

by Deborah Rozman, Ph.D.

D0882106

Aslan Publishing
Planetary Publications
Boulder Creek, California

Aslan Publishing
Planetary Publications
14795 West Park Ave.
Boulder Creek, CA 95006

Rozman, Deborah.
    Meditation for children: pathways to happiness,
    harmony, creativity and fun for the family /
    Deborah Rozman. --2nd ed.
    p. cm.

ISBN 0-944031-25-0 (paperback)
ISBN 0-944031-31-5 (hardback)
        1. Meditation. 2. Children -- Religious life. 3. Family --
Religious life. I. Title.
BL627.R69   1989
158' . 12'082--dc20   89-37747 CIP

© 1976, Deborah Rozman
© 1989, Deborah Rozman

First Edition, University of the Trees Press, 1976
Second Edition, Aslan Publishing, 1989

All rights reserved. No part of this publication may be
reproduced, stored in a retrieval system or transmitted in any form
or by any means, electronic, mechanical, photocopy, recording or
otherwise, without prior written permission from Aslan Publishing, 310
Blue Ridge Dr., Boulder Creek, California, USA, with the exception of
short excerpts used with acknowledgement of publisher and author.

The Acknowledgement section of this book
is considered to be a part of the copyright notice.

Printed in USA

10 9 8 7 6 5 4 3 2 1

CONTENTS

Foreword

This book is an introduction to a new lifestyle of family living and child rearing geared to evolutionary change. Its purpose and goal is to bring greater love, truth, integrity and fulfillment to every being by helping all, young and old, to be more in touch with their true Self.

Hopefully, experiences like those provided here which cut through the delusions and ignorances that cloud human beings, will help transform living into more of a cooperative, creative expression. Buried and repressed feelings and thoughts produce negative energy which manifests in mistrust and destructive conflict between people, and unfulfilled lives. Cleansing and clearing ourselves from this negativity in creative ways and keeping ourselves and our loved ones clear, makes conflict constructive, and puts us in touch with our true being.

The fun games and experiences provided in this book can be used by those new to the fields of meditation and self-discovery, or by those already practicing some form of guided meditation. Everyone can learn to broaden and deepen love and trust in life experience. In order to refine consciousness and dissolve the little personality into the Universal Consciousness which is latent in all humans, we learn to dissolve the ego membrane of insecurity (the self-sense that separates us from other people all of whom have egos of their own). *Creative* conflict rubs away the separative membrane.

The confusion and disorder in our world today is made from the confusion and disorder in the individuals who make up our world, and it is with us as individuals that world transformation must begin. While there are many forms of meditation available for adults, there is little that I know of other than my previous book, *Meditating With Children*, designed to be used in the classroom or with groups of children, which is directed toward fulfilling children's needs. Nor is there anything, to my knowledge, in the way of a comprehensive program for applying meditation to the family or group living situation. This book is written to fill these lacks. Certainly our family and group living is the blueprint for our larger social groups. Any family, any person, who lives or works with others, any group of people living or working together, can benefit from this real and in depth way of living. We now have the tools available to transform human consciousness on a large scale, on our little planet, in this huge universe.

Deborah Rozman
Boulder Creek, California

Acknowledgements

I'd like to acknowledge all the people past and present at the University of the Trees community who contributed so much to my spiritual growth. And especially to Christopher Hills who inspired so many of the meditations and games and ideas in the first edition of this book.

I'd like to thank the wonderful children in our family, whose radiant faces are on the cover of this new edition, for the delightful people that they are and for the joy of discovering the treasures of life with them.

There are over 200,000 books in print between the six printings to date of my first book, *Meditating With Children: The Art of Concentration and Centering* (for groups and classrooms) and the six printings including mass market edition of *Meditation for Children* (for individuals and families). Both these books were written in the mid 1970's. Hundreds of people have written to me on the benefits they and their children have received from them. Although meditation is ageless, my hope is that this new edition will bring even greater peace and happiness to many thousands more in the 1990's. The only extensive changes in this new edition are the dedication, and the new Chapter 0. But from my point of view, they are the most important part of the book, setting a new tone for a new decade.

Deborah Rozman
1989

Front cover children: Erin White and Christian Paddison
Back cover children: Joshua Jonas and Elysia Joy Cryer

Line drawings: Mary Ann Bruno

Dedication

I dedicated my first book, *Meditating With Children: The Art of Concentration and Centering* to the "Universal Mother of Compassion who willingly responds to the call of the child." When I finally met her, in the heart of peace, I found Mom was all compassion and also a lot of fun. In fact it seems like she loves fun and play and happiness more than anything. It grows us better. So naturally she wants all her kids, big and little, to become stress-free, to have that inner peace that will take them to and keep them in that child-like spirit of ever more playful fun and delight – on lots of levels and in new ways we've never thought of before, because she loves surprises and, I believe, so do we all.

It's in this childlike spirit that I dedicate my new edition of *Meditation For Children* to Mom, and to my very best buddy, Lew Childre, who brought Mom to me in the heart of hearts and in real life, and has shown me and my friends an entire new and ever-changing reality of fun – ever expanding – and totally redefining the meaning and purpose of meditation.

Nursery Rhyme for Mom – Who Loves Surprises

Young Mom Funster
Really was a punster.
She loved her children way big.
She strode into town
Wiped away every frown
And showed them an ever new gig.

Young Mom Funster
Herself e're a youngster,
Loved her children way deep.
She liked more to play
Than she ever would say,
To laugh and to dance and to leap.

Young Mom Funster
A true all-for-onester,
Showed her kids a neat trick.
If you care from the heart
but not overcare e'en a part,
Your life will be real smooth and slick.

Young Mom Funster
Raised hell like a gunster,
'cause she found ol' heaven a bore.
She wanted buddies to play with
Not fuddy duddy's to stay with,
Buddies totally fulfilled to the core.

Young Mom Funster,
With more magic than a munster,
wants all her children complete.
None more special than another,
Truly sister and brother,
And that is the way biggest treat.

Chapter 0

Funtasia – The Next Reality

Since I first wrote this book in 1976, my own spiritual growth has been filled with a kaleidoscope of changing perspectives which have unfolded into a whole new level of fun. I discovered that when life begins with stress-free, care-free peace, it takes on new textures of enjoyment, ecstasies, discoveries, colorations of delight and deeper joy. But best of all it takes on a quality of buddyhood – a kind of friendship with others that I only felt once in a while with my very best friends when I was a child, with a special person I could trust and confide in, or when I felt truly in love.

The fun factor is the light factor, the delight factor, that the quiet of meditation brings forth from the deepest heart place and lights up, bubbling through our personality into daily life. We become more free to experience our natural and spontaneous childlike spirit. Life from the heart bubbles forth as spontaneous rhyme and rhythm, a delight in life's many conveniences guiding the boats of our souls down a river of secure fun and peace. Even the ups and downs, which of course come at times when we encounter the white waters of life's turbulence, have an inner rhythm that protects, even while they scare, and in the end help us become a more caring and carefree person.

So what ultimate use is any method, or meditation, any game or any knowledge, if it's not to delight in becoming more of who we really are, more of our true self and the goodness it is, and sharing that with others? When we meet the fears and traumas, those monsters in our life adventure, we can face them with hope and be victorious more quickly. Whether the lumps and bumps that slump us every so often are little or big, we can be our own hero and transform those growing pains into fun with our buddies – in family, school, and friends. The purpose of *Meditation for Children* is to give us an inner environment with as little stress as possible from which to direct our life course. Meditation is the compass to guide us to as smooth a life rhythm as we can experience. It does so by enhancing our intuitive sensitivities to the frequencies of life in and around us (energies, images, thoughts, feelings and sensations are all frequencies) and deepening our heartfelt connections with people and with life. As we become more sensitive and stronger in our heart we add new dimensions, levels and layers of meaning to true fun.

Poem to Fun:

Funtasia for All Ages

Fluffles and Bubbles, Squiggles and Qum
Shhhhsh's and squeals of giggles spell fun.
Jumping on pillows, soaking up sun,
Best buddies all together and just one on one.
Textures and feel goods like mmm'ss and yumm's
Ahhh's and Oooh's, teehees and hummms.
Tastes and sounds, smells and sights,
tickles and nibbles, aprons and kites.
All by myself, dancing in the grass,
Looking at stars or prancing real fast.
Quiet as a mouse or curling up in bed,
Making believe or dreaming instead.

I love to play games to see really wide,
and have the funniest, kushiest ride
to new parts of me and new parts of you,
growing forever and being a kid too.

You can have your cake and eat it too,
'cause what would cake be if it wasn't for you?

So what's the real reason to meditate? To have more fun, whatever that truly is for you. And you may not even know what that is yet. More thrills in your cells – enjoyment of your soul – fulfillment in your heart. Sometimes we have to start to stop – or stop to start – or move to get comfy – or be still to get a good aim. That's why life is like a game. Here's some ways we can learn without getting burned from overthinking and overtrying in our heads and frying in our mistakes. We can be light and bright so we can all win and bingo – do it right.

How can *Meditation for Children* help get the kinks out of the flows of our relationships? By giving us a doorway into ourself. Then from our deeper center we move into life, and magnetize more fun into it – intuit. Can you imagine discovering this new reality with someone else? What a buddy you would have. More kinds of play together, daring, caring, sharing, deeply touching times together, real heart intimacy that empowers your soul and brings forth the best in everyone you meet. Meditation brings in light and helps us get truly objective in our subjective universe. In other words, by surrendering to our heart and caring from our heart, but not over-caring (because we are detached in our perspective at the same time), we draw in light and become light and that changes our perspective to something wider and always better.

When we're light, we can be silly, spontaneous, sweet or sometimes mischievous, always in a good spirit, always childlike in our freedom. And light is energy, power,

intelligence. Then the more energy and power, the more
light and bright and free we are.

> Light and bright
> Filled our sight
> And we took off
> Like a bird in flight.
> Our hearts way widened
> Everyone inside 'em
> Feeling so right
> We didn't need to fight
> or live in fright
> of others' might.

So this new chapter in my life and new addition or edition
to this book is not to take anything away from where it's
been and what it contains, but to add to. To add to it more
heart, more frequencies of possibility and hope and energy.
Fun, fluff and delight do help speed us along our journey to
completion and fulfillment of our earth experience. And I
hope that all who pick up this book will be able to move a
little more sprightly and peacefully along their journey to
harmony and richer fun.

Sometimes the idea of peace can seem boring. We like
thrill and excitement because it seems more fun. Sometimes
even love seems sentimental, and harmony sounds like dull
angels playing violins on clouds, when our idea of fun is
sport or passion or tenderness or a poignant heart touch.
And even the word fun, while always uplifting, can seem to
mean something superficial, like the froth on the wave and
we want the soul-stirring depth and power of the ocean too.

Well, all these are textures of life, and the doorway to all
the designer textures and experiences we like or desire or
dream of, is in finding our way through everyday life with
minimum stress and maximum convenience and fulfillment.
And that starts with inner peace and harmonious relating
with others. The meditations and awareness games practiced
in this handbook can help you with that. By helping you

find your own deeper center of inner security you change your perspective and deepen your experience of all the other textures of life, whether sensations or insights, visions, knowledge, grace, happy surprises or any true heart's desire fulfilled. The pot of gold at the rainbow's end is real – it's in your pure heart crystal in your heart of hearts, and therein lies everything fulfilling you can dream of and then some.

So this new edition is to lift your attitude towards meditation beyond any old idea of just a technique or a discipline or having to sit still, or something religious or clinically scientific. It's to give you a new shot in the heart – of fluff and fun – a new frequency to approach your life with and really have the hope that a sense of completion in the heart can be yours and your children's. The best attitude I was taught and learned to like to practice because of its immediate rewards, in terms of fun and joy and bliss and insight, was to care from the heart about others and at the same time *not* care about getting caught up in my moods or views about what is or isn't. Then I find they change to something lighter and better if I don't get hung up in them. That brings a level of trust in the universe and surrender in the heart flow that I only dreamed of before. This kind of "not caring", allows me to let go and let the flow move my heartsong along faster and easier than if I get caught up in the heady whys and wherefores of every funky thing I think or feel. And hey presto, the right insight comes and I'm free of that.

True caring, on the other hand, includes making times to really share with myself what's going on with me in meditation, or sharing something that I'm caught up in overcaring about with a buddy before it turns into a worse funky feeling or mood. That bails me or my buddy out of that energy glitch more quickly than anything else I've found. When we can be buddies together, not to despair together, but to get out of perspectives that don't feel great and aren't productive, like anger and frustration-stress, and into the soft heart together, then aren't we really getting to the heart of what heaven on earth really could be like? This is no idealistic pie in the sky concept. My extended familyand I have proved it out for ourselves and we and our children live happy lives and are getting happier.

As children or as adults many of us had at one time or other, that best buddy we could tell anything to, even the most intimate things and feel totally accepted. If we didn't have that buddy, we were probably wishing for it and maybe even looking longingly for it, either in a teacher, a friend, a pet, a mate, a clergyman, a therapist or in just that special someone. We were reaching out for that part of ourself that wants to feel complete and whole so that we can be more of ourself and then guess what? We can have more fun, play more with each other, discover new things about the universe together, explore more of life more abundantly.

So meditation is not an end in itself. Sometimes it's a paddleboard to ease our swim across the lake of life. Sometimes it's a life raft to carry us through turbulent times, and other times it's a surfboard or even jet skis to skim across the waters into new fun-filled dimensions of awareness that we have only let ourself dream about before or glimpsed or experienced for short periods of time. But best of all, it can help take us to that heart center of the universe that we did not even know was there waiting to fulfill us more deeply than our deepest dreams.

When you approach the exercises or games in this book, if you are feeling light already, great, they will make you feel even better. If you want to reduce your stress or change your mood, use them to help you. If you have a problem with someone, try doing something fun together first, laugh and be bubbly if you can, so you can let some fresh energy and light in and don't get all worried and overcaring about what was bothering you. Then, talk about whatever you feel is unresolved; don't ignore it or it will bring you down again. Use the active listening exercises, meditate together or play some of the awareness games together and watch your friendships grow into ones of real buddyhood. That's all for this edition. Until the next......

Chapter 1

What is Meditation?

The word meditation comes from a Sanskrit word, *medha,* which means wisdom. Medha-tation means doing the wisdom, getting in touch with the wisdom inside oneself. It becomes a guide for dealing with everyday problems and situations successfully. Through meditating we learn to "tune in" so we can be wise in everything we do. This guidance is available to everyone because it is part of each person's nature, just as the mind, feelings and senses are part of each person. Like a hidden gold mine it is untapped in most people, but those who know how to contact it have a great wealth that is always there for them to use.

Much of the knowledge from which we draw, in learning to use meditation to get in touch with this great wisdom inside us, comes from Eastern meditators, many Hindu or Buddhist, who have researched deeply into the soul. They generally agree that the soul is balanced by the law of cause and effect. That it reaps all the effects of actions it has sown and thereby gains wisdom from them. They believe all difficult situations are unconquered challenges for growth. The word they use to describe this is *karma,* which is the force generated by a person's actions that causes and per-

petuates reactions and transmigration. In its ethical consequences karma determines the soul's destiny in its next
existence.

Through these causes and effects the intelligence of each
person is finally evolved to the point where it foresees the
consequences of its actions and so acts with true wisdom. It
is surrendered to a selfless awareness that guides the will to
the right course. When tempted to act in a certain way that
will bring pain, it says no, based on experience and foresight. Wisdom comes when hindsight becomes foresight.
When its earthly lessons are completed the soul's love becomes pure. It will not be able to harm another nor can it be
harmed by another. When this stage of liberation is
achieved then we have a true seer and Son of God.

In the West we more frequently are told, do unto others
as you would have them do unto you. The western religions
haven't emphasized that this works on the level of thought
and imagining as well as physically.

Meditators who have studied human nature say if we
image and think something that will be hurtful to another
the hurt will eventually come back to us. The energy law
that every action has an equal and opposite reaction is also
a spiritual law and applies to our thoughts and actions as
well as to physical energy. If we program something hurtful
we will at sometime receive something hurtful to teach us
that everyone is our Self and part of the One. Equally,
when we program something positive and helpful we will
receive and be helped by it.

The evolving soul is like a vibrating vortex of energy—
vibrating with its psychological tendencies and unfulfilled
desires.It is attracted to situations so that it can have the
most fertile environment for being confronted with them to
work through them.

In meditation we learn to contact our inner wisdom by
quieting our bodies, our feelings and our thoughts. It is only
when we quiet these activites of our personality that go on
most of the time and get them out of the way that our Real
Self can surface. Then we become very clear, and in that

clarity the needed answers come. We may not know how these answers come or where they come from but we feel an inner sense of certainty about our Self. This is an extremely fulfilling experience and life takes on deeper meaning. We become more aware in whatever we do.

Some people wonder if meditation is contrary to their religious beliefs. Actually it is very similar to "going into the silence" or to prayer which most religions teach. It helps to think of meditation as a healthy psychological tool for contacting our spiritual nature. It can be used by any person from any walk of life, any religion, any country or any age.

Most people who meditate find that regular practice is the most beneficial. The length of time will vary with personal needs. For families with small children who want to meditate together, five to ten minutes a day to start is a good length. With very young children the time may have to be reduced to two or three minutes until concentration becomes more developed. But even this short period of deep relaxation will have wonderful results. As the desire to experience inner peace and its benefits grows with practice, the meditation time will increase. It is the quality of contact with the inner peace, clarity, joy and love that comes from the Real Self within that is important. Thirty minutes to an hour of meditation, once or twice daily, is very common for those who have practiced for a time, including children.

For beginners, the procedure of meditation, briefly, is as follows: (You may want to put these instructions on a tape recorder and then listen to them.)

Sit upright in a comfortable position with the spine and back straight, yet relaxed. Close the eyes. Relax the body. Do this by tensing the left foot. Let it go. Tense the right foot. Let it go. Relax all the nerves and muscles. Tense the left calf and let it go. Tense the right calf and let it go. Relax each part of the body completely.

Continue with the left thigh, then the right thigh, the left buttocks, right buttocks, abdomen and stomach, left chest, right chest, left forearm and hand, right forearm and hand, left upper arm, right upper arm, left shoulder, right shoulder, neck, face, head and scalp muscles.

Now, take a deep breath and let all the tensions or pent up feelings go. Feel limp, and relaxed. The body is still, the emotions and feelings are calm.

Now relax the mind, and let it go. Look within, inwards and up without straining the eyes. Imagine a point between the eyebrows inside the forehead. Focus all the attention at this point and concentrate, but stay relaxed. If thoughts come in just let them pass through, bringing the attention back to the point of concentration between the eyebrows inside the head. Gently continue to bring the attention back every time it wanders. Practice this for a few minutes. Now see if you can feel the heart beating. Become aware of the rhythmic breath. Soon we begin to experience a very peaceful, nice feeling of being centered inside ourself. It is from this center that we receive a fresh supply of energy and awareness.

This is basically what occurs. More complete instructions and techniques are found in the following chapters. The feeling of being centered and aware remains even after the meditation period is over. It can be felt as we go about our daily routine, whether washing dishes, doing schoolwork, pounding a nail or relating with others.

The more we meditate the more this experience of being centered is with us throughout the day.

It is difficult for a child to do much with meditation until he has learned a little self-discipline, but the results it brings are well worth the initial patience and effort. It becomes very rewarding to the child's self-image. He is becoming a master of himself when he can quiet his body, emotions and thoughts to experience the deep center. The child gains a strong sense of inner authority; questions are answered from within. In the joy, sense of well-being and direct perception that opens up, the child gains self-reliance and can do better in whatever he is interested. The gradual development of deep concentration that goes with meditation becomes part of his character. Then the vibrant and often scattered energy of childhood becomes directed and used, by the child himself, to achieve his own goals.

Chapter 2

Meditation as an Individual Affair

COMMUNING WITH YOUR INNER SELF

The only way to really know what meditation is, is to do it. We are going to explore meditation now as the ultimate love affair with our true Self. It is important to directly experience meditation and have a taste of what we are talking about. Read the next two paragraphs, then go back to the simple instructions for beginning meditation and actually begin the first step of meditating. This exercise will put you more in tune with what is to follow by tuning your mind into a new frequency.

When you have gone as deep within as you can this first time, just stay there— in that peaceful, calm center— and ask yourself the profound question, Who am I? With eyes still closed, in the meditative state, contemplate whatever comes into your awareness. Wait a little and then ask again. Who am I? Keep asking yourself this question in the calm center and consider the answer, or lack of answer, for awhile.

Meditating on the very basic question of Who am I? is where we begin our new adventure in discovering the Source of our own existence. Insights will come. Be expectant, but don't be discouraged if you don't recognize anything new immediately. It often takes a great deal of practice and willpower just to learn to sit quietly no matter how old we are. We are used to running restless thoughts in our minds and making excuses for ourselves about other things we should be doing. Watch the mind and its tricks as it tries to wiggle out of this simple discipline.

It is a well-known scientific fact that the average person is using only about ten to fifteen percent of his brain cells at this time in history. Try to imagine the potential in the other eighty-five to ninety percent that are not being used! They are lying dormant, like a bear hibernating. Humanity has very little idea of what may be possible in this untapped awareness potential. There is no way of knowing, except through those few who have awakened to a larger percentage of it in themselves. Meditation and other awareness-expanding exercises awaken dormant brain cells. The energy we receive as we meditate stimulates the brain neurons, increasing their capacity to allow more awareness to enter the indwelling consciousness.

It is very easy to talk about nature or the laws of the universe that man experiences through his five senses. But to know the Self who makes sense of what our eyes, ears, taste, touch and smell, together with what our feelings and thoughts tell us, is not very common. We usually take our own awareness for granted and only a very few people have ever bothered to do the meditation that takes them deeper into the real nature of their perceptions. Those that do, experience how the Self connects with energy, light, consciousness, other people, and God the Creator.

Such an investigation into the nature of the Self by individuals on a worldwide scale, is the real New Age which is dawning in the minds of many adults who are seeking spiritual reality. The earlier we introduce our children to this great adventure in Self-discovery, the more prepared they will be to lead the world into a new stage of evolution.

Meditating on Who am I? by going to the source within, is a key to this new awakening. It unlocks the prison house of our own blindness enabling us to perceive beyond the limited personality. Our inner awareness opens up a new faculty of direct knowing which transcends mind, emotions and senses, and sees nature in its essence and human situations clear, just as they really are.

The personality acts as a filter to this direct perception. No two personalities are the same, and there are different levels of awareness that make up each personality. The diagram below is like the True Self, the Center within, with seven different levels of awareness which work as filters to color our experiences. Each person functions mostly in one or two of the levels although we each have all of them. The True Self can only be discovered directly; it cannot be known with any of these faculties since it is beyond them all. But we need to learn to develop these levels to discover the Self. The realization that man is equipped with these different levels of perceiving came to sages who were in direct contact with the center within and could see through the human world of experience. Many scientists have been shocked at the amount of brain activity in the tests performed on some of these exceptional people.

The seven levels of Awareness

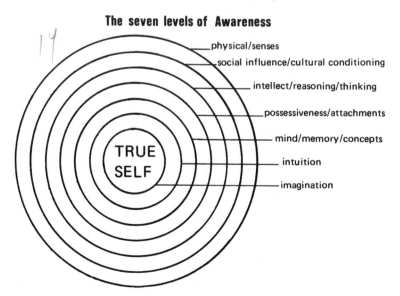

Each of these levels of awareness produces a different energy in the form of a different color, like the seven colors of the rainbow. The colors can be seen in the aura (the energy field around the body). Some adults and many children can see auras if they learn to shift their eye focus a bit. The aura colors show the levels of consciousness going on inside the person. Exercises to see aura colors are on page 133 of this book. In most people these levels are not clear. Awareness of the different levels is usually vague. Do you know on which level (s) you mainly live? On which level(s) your children mainly live? As the levels become clear they can be likened to a sun filtering through a clear prism producing a beautiful rainbow of seven pure colors. Other people's levels will become obvious too. No wonder this purifying process is called en*light*enment. Most marriage and family problems occur because the members function on different levels and don't know what to do about it. So their communication is like this ⇌; they don't really meet nor do they understand where the other is coming from.

The meditation process helps us expand to include other levels of awareness in addition to the ones we usually use. If we relate to the world through thinking, we may find our Self becoming more intuitive or more sensitive. If we are basically imaginative we may need to get our feet on the ground and become more practical. We get more energy to be whatever we already are and to become more of what we want to be. New ideas and images of who we really are and what we can do open up to the inner consciousness. We find our Self growing in ways we never learn in school, work or normal family living. We will soon find we are able to relate to more types of people.

As meditation practice increases the rewards increase. Everyone receives calmness, insights, energy and bliss feelings from the same Source, but each person manifests them differently through the personality. While we meditate to go beyond personality, we also develop our unique individuality. Our personal talents and skills become energized.

For example, if you like to play the piano, expanded awareness will help you to become a much finer pianist. Awareness of the whole being is expanded as energy flows through all the levels, and whatever you do becomes more meaningful. Even tasks that used to be boring become more pleasant.

The more insights we gain into how the personality filters life, the closer we get to the Center within. Our meditations grow deeper and more fulfilling the closer we get. *Know thyself* is the human evolutionary motto, and is the task before each person and before humanity as a whole. Each individual must use his own free will to research into himself, no one else can do it for him. It is beyond all ideology— communist, socialist, capitalist— because it means facing yourself *as you are*, not as you or the society believes you ought to be. No social revolution can enlighten man. It can only provide the education and life conditions whereby each man can go within to discover the patterning which blocks him from the enlightened state. We can have a real enlightened state when enough people concentrate on making this discovery, not before. We might think we are able to see through our society now, but can we see how deeply society has colored our own personal thoughts and values— inside? Ask yourself.

How can we learn to recognize our own filters? We must learn to trace down the causes of our own problems and disturbances. Until we do we cannot be certain of the truth of our perceptions. Very few people are actually aware of the traps in their own ways of thinking and seeing. We have to go beyond our normal ways of looking in order to even see our own traps. Easterners use an analogy of a fish in water. A fish cannot know what water is because it is always in it. Similarly man does not know what the traps of the mind are because he's always caught in the mind. Some other faculty beyond the mind needs awakening to be able to see through the mind.

Scientists have studied nature using the five senses, many instruments and mathematics. But how the scientist's mind and beliefs affect his observations has not really been investigated. In fact, scientists make every effort to divorce their own consciousness from what is being observed. But they can never be totally successful because it always takes the mind to interpret the experimental results. And the mind is always colored by its previous experiences.

Eventually not only science, but politics, religion, sociology, indeed every field, is going to have to come to terms with the way human consciousness works. Even if two thousand people see everything the same, it doesn't necessarily make it true because someone with greater wisdom and perception might come along and provide a new insight that will prove the way those two thousand people were seeing to be false. This is what happened when Galileo proved the world was round, not flat. This is what happened when Albert Einstein brought the theory of relativity to science. Many scientists had to admit that what they previously believed was true, from their sense observations and their way of thinking, was not true.

This is what happened when Christ and other seers have brought fresh inspiration to the world. Man has had to ditch some of his old notions. The problem with most humans is that we ignorantly assume that our minds perceive truth and that we're seeing correctly. But this is not the case. We operate with false basic assumptions and these basic assumptions that we make have created most of the conflict between individuals and between societies in the world today and throughout history. To really evolve awareness we have to look into our blocks to awareness. We have to see how basic assumptions in our minds cause problems.

Basic assumptions act as filters. It is as if we are looking at the world through a mirror and so we see our own assumptions reflected back to us as reality. Or, to use another analogy, looking through rose-colored glasses makes all the world look rose. We assume it is a rosy world we live in. Delving into and confronting our filters in day-to-day living is just as essential for true meditation as sitting in the still center. This type of awareness expansion is called meditation in action.

Let's look at an example from daily life of how filters work to color our seeing.

Jim and John are looking at each other through their own mind filters. Jim is really a greedy person but doesn't know it. By looking through his filter mirror, he thinks others are greedy. Jim sees his own filter of greed mirrored back to him when he looks at John, so he develops a basic assumption that John is greedy. This feeling is triggered by John asking for something.

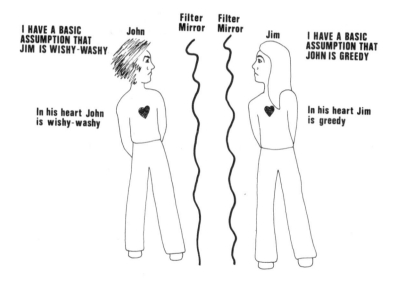

I HAVE A BASIC ASSUMPTION THAT JIM IS WISHY-WASHY   John   Filter Mirror   Filter Mirror   Jim   I HAVE A BASIC ASSUMPTION THAT JOHN IS GREEDY

In his heart John is wishy-washy

In his heart Jim is greedy

John is really wishy-washy and doesn't know it. He sees Jim as wishy-washy through his filter mirror. John believes Jim is wishy-washy because Jim hesitates. "Man, you've got to keep on that guy to get an answer. He can't make decisions at all," says John. John's wife, however, will tell you John is twice as bad.

These assumptions get *projected* back and forth onto the other. John becomes very greedy in Jim's eyes and Jim very wishy-washy in John's eyes when it is really much more the other way around. Then each gets hopping mad by their own unknown fault which they see and judge in the other. Confusion and miscommunication result! Each picks up on the other's anger vibes, thereby reinforcing the anger. Both leave, feeling uptight and mad at the other.

Projection

To summarize, our filters serve as mirrors for our own problems, but we generally think we're seeing the other's problem. This is called the mirror effect. Whenever we find ourself judging another we need to learn to point the finger at ourself to see if the fault is in us too. Now, it may be in the other more than in us, but we have to learn to look within first, before judging. A good clue to go by is: if what we are seeing in someone else disturbs us, then there is probably a problem for us to work on in ourself. "John and Jim" discussions go on between everyone in differing degrees. We can watch it happening between two children calling each other names, between two adults arguing.

This illustration was very simple. Usually there is even more to unravel because, not only do we look through our own filter at the other, but we sometimes experience the other's filter looking back at us too. The other's filter includes the other person's image of himself and his image of us which may or may not be true. These impressions add more color to our own coloring. For example, if someone gets mad at us we may say, "Gee, am I really that bad? Is

Freak out!

he seeing right? Am I seeing right? Who's right?" Some people trust others' judgments more than their own. This is called *identification*— identifying with the other. Some people outright reject others' perceptions about them. Both are incorrect. The real need is to understand and learn to perceive the filter-mirroring process.

To say it all another.way, it is as if we look through filters of images, intuitions, memories, ideas, thoughts, fears, hopes, desires, cultural conditioning and other stereotypes that we have acquired while growing up and living in society. These stereotypes condition the way we see events, objects, nature and especially other people who have filters too. Because we are looking through this glass darkly we end up seeing darkness and believe that's the way the other really is. We end up *projecting* our own filters into what we see and into what others see without even knowing it.

Getting into the complexity of man's consciousness is like getting into gooey quicksand unless we can use some skill and direct perception to cut right through. Searching out our basic assumptions, projections and identifications can enable us to slice through the confusion. Let's look at some more examples.

Basic Assumptions: A wife may assume that because her husband didn't phone from work to say he was going to be late that he is up to some hanky-panky or he has gotten into an accident so she worries her head off. Or a child assumes that because his teacher didn't call on him first today, like yesterday, and seemed to look at him a little funny that she doesn't like him anymore. These impressions are very subtle. From what insecurities do they stem? As children, insecurity may have been picked up from *identifying* with a parental insecurity. Consciousness becomes very intertwined between people. A person may also assume they have the greatest teacher, lover, leader, master or guru in the world because they have *identified* so closely with his teachings or with the good feelings they get from him that they don't see; they become blind to anything or anyone else.

Everyone has probably experienced this at one time or another, when, blindly, we feel *our way* is the best way, or the only way. And the more love and consciousness we invest in *our way*, the more is going to come back to us, of course, reinforcing our good feelings. Love grows in this manner, but the danger is in not seeing the process and becoming blind and judgmental toward *other ways*.

Projections: A wife may, unconsciously, want to spend some time just getting to know male friends other than her own husband. When she sees her husband glance at another woman, she *assumes* that he would like to do the same. She projects her own feelings onto him and gets jealous, giving him a cold shoulder when he really was only admiring the woman's smile. Rarely do these filtered situations come out in the open. They just cause funny feelings inside or build up into resentments. To bring them out might be like opening Pandora's box. But with techniques to guide us, it can be done constructively.

Identification: A young woman watches TV and identifies with the lover in the soap opera who has lost her love. She starts to cry with her just as if it was her own loss. Or, a father identifies with and is moved by a friend who is having trouble with his family. He comes back home and lets out the frustration he picked up on his own family.

Identification is not in itself good or bad. It depends on what we do with it. It is a natural mechanism that can help us develop sensitivity to others, but if we are weak it will pull us off our own center into the other's center and color us more.

A child may sit hypnotized for hours every night in front of the TV identifying with the feelings of the characters. He laughs while some silly dumb cartoon fellow gets banged on the head by a cartoon animal for doing something stupid. This type of identification may develop a sense of humor, but too much can develop callousness. The child may get scared in his guts at some monster movie, or have nightmares about being shot and strangled, picked up from a weekly police series he saw on TV just before bed, where he identified with the victim. All of these identifications condition consciousness and create filters.

We can't hide from life to prevent negative conditioning, but we can learn to center ourself more and learn how to see through the mirroring/filtering process. It may seem a hard or even hopeless task to transcend filters, but when we realize that we must start with ourself and observe how thoughts and feelings arise and what causes them in us, we begin to make headway.

The meditation in the still center is essential to help us get beyond the filters and light them up for us to see. It is the most important tool we can use to Center. The joy that comes with the unfolding self-discovery is its own reward and actually makes our awakening and clearing process very beautiful. Understanding and compassion for those still blind to themselves comes to us as we grow.

Even beginners can use meditation right away to help solve disturbing problems as they arise. Let's use an example to illustrate. Our best friend, Bob, has some habits that really bother us, make us angry. He often borrows clothes or money and forgets to return what we have loaned. We have to remind him several times before we finally get back what is ours. Instead of getting upset as usually happens, we catch our thoughts and use our will to meditate. We breathe deeply to relax our angered feelings and our restless and tense body that is uptight because of the anger and resentment. We stop our mind that is circling round and round, worrying about our money or our sweater, wondering if we should say something stronger this time, or worrying that if we do get heavier Bob may no longer like us. Normally the mind repeats over and over with one concern after another, like a tape recorder in the head, until we make a decision either to take some action or forget it. Then the tricky mind might just shift to another track based upon what action we take. If we tell Bob off, the mind might start to really race with worry and guilt about having hurt his feelings. The mind has so many patterns. So we meditate to relieve ourself from all these patterns for awhile. We let it all go and are free of it. For those moments we are not clogged by basic assumptions, projections, identifications or personal reactions and attitudes. In other words, we get out of our little self and its filters and are no longer disturbed. Then in this clear, peaceful space inside we see something more about Bob and why he does these things. We also see more about ourself and why we get so upset and still keep lending him things. We see through the situation and then the solution comes clearly into our awareness. In this instance we realize that Bob is just very absentminded and that we really do like him as a friend. He has a lot of other good qualities and means no harm. We decide that it really isn't so bad after all. We also see, although it is uncomfortable to look at, our own strong attachment to money and clothes which is coloring our opinion of Bob. In this new light we no longer see him as greedy. We realize that was a projection. So we feel better because we have a clearer view of the situation. We decide to share the experience with Bob and to our surprise it brings the two of us closer. We have touched truth and gained wisdom about ourself and Bob.

Each time we solve a problem in this manner we strengthen our own inner conviction and self-respect. Now some people may say, "Well, I'm already doing that without meditation." But until we can do this all the time, until we have total mastery over our ego-personality, our mind, feelings and restless body and can get beyond them and their filters at will, we still need mediation as a tool to achieve this mastery.

The wonder of meditation is that we can experience some transcending of filters, some peace or good feeling, right from the start. Glimpses into higher intelligence, love, high energy or power attributed to the Source by wise seers and prophets will come as we continue to meditate. It is this contact that gives us the fuel and the fulfillment to continue toward discovering ourselves. Very gradually we enter into that *central sun* within as we unfold ourself to ourself. This is the meaning of self-realization. The mind becomes clear and stops getting in our way.

To use the words of one great teacher, "Meditation is developing your own hotline to the infinite."

As we continue to meditate, we at times wonder if our experiences, or the answers that come to our problems, are inspired by the higher self or whether they are not just a product of one of our cloudy filters. How do we know the answers are real wisdom? The only way we can know is to test them out and see if they work in our daily life. It is no use to just assume they are truth. While they may seem true from our point of view, from a more enlightened viewpoint they may not be true at all— they may just be some identification with a good feeling, or some assumption. But we have to start from where we are, and the best way is to see if they really work in our living situations. As they work out we learn to trust our inner knowledge. When they don't work out we have to find out why. One way of finding out is to take a problem that is puzzling you, that you have been unable to resolve. Use meditation and go into the center within, beyond your present thoughts by the method given in Chapter 1 or by another method that works for you. In the stillest part ask your True Self for the real answer or solution. Be open to receive whatever idea enters and write down all that comes to you. Don't start to doubt or question yet, wait until it is all out. Afterwards examine the answer. It still may be a product of your filters. But if it feels possible test it out all the same. After some practice you will know when you get a true answer because there is a certainty and a feeling of release that comes with it. However, it takes practice to recondition the consciousness. Just think how long we have spent conditioning it.

Some typical life problems for many adults and children are boredom and unfulfillment. We look for stimulation in parties, games, TV, drugs, etc., to keep from being bored with ourselves. Meditation provides an inner stimulus that is not just a diversion like TV or an escape like most drugs. It stimulates our inner creative potential as it works to dissolve the personality filters. We gradually learn to identify with the Source rather than with the personality. Often non-meditators have attacked meditation as something only confused people with problems do. This type of statement is also a misconception. While it is true that many people have gone to meditation as a means of solving deep problems, it is ignorant to assume that meditation is only for the confused. It may be that people attracted to meditation are more acutely aware of the problems and confusions that beset human consciousness and are determined to get to the causes and correct them. Many people have an image of meditators as individuals who escape from involvement with life and society. But this is also a misconception of the real role of meditation in the evolutionary process. Its real purpose is to enable us to see into life and society and to provide us with energy and illumination to solve its problems.

As personal problems begin to get solved, the consciousness is freed to experience more of its universal nature, less of the obsessive little self and its personality. Let's experience this nature.

At the next opportunity, now, if possible, go outdoors and sit comfortably for awhile just looking at the grass. Imagine yourself becoming the grass. Feel grassness. Experience yourself moving in the wind. The grass seems brighter, it has character of its own. Feel your greenness— sparkly and light— and maybe there is a suggestion of coolness or wetness, even though it may be in the heat of the day. Commune with the life in the grass and experience its purity. Experience its oneness with the life in yourself. Stay with this for awhile until it becomes real for you. Here we have communed with the Source, which is the same in the grass as it is in us. We can now expand our awareness and be in touch with that same Source as it pours through other aspects of creation, the trees, the birds, etc., lighting them from within, and revealing their true nature to us. Do this simple exercise slowly and thoroughly.

When we are bored or frustrated we are cut off from the inner contact with our true self. Then of course we are cut off from the one Source which links us with everything and everyone else. Life will seem meaningless and will not be fulfilling— we will not be filled full with love or joy.

With meditation we have the key to turn on the life force anytime we want. We just clear away our filters temporarily and make room for life to flow into us. The Source is always there waiting for us to tap it and develop our potential. It is like going on a real adventure. We don't know ahead of time what is going to happen. While it's good to expect growth we must be aware not to block the flow by being impatient. Impatience and frustration are also filters. And remember, meditation only works as well as we who do it can forget our little separate personal selves. It becomes the ultimate love affair, since it brings us to union with the true Self, the One in ourself and in others. We develop deep devotion to this One when we realize that it is the One who is in all, loves us through all and loves all through us.

As we begin our new love affair we need to be made aware of the pitfalls that every meditator encounters at one time or another. While we can be very idealistic about the potentials of meditation, these will only be experienced if we are, at the same time, very realistic about the process.

Sometimes we may feel, Ugh! I don't want to meditate today. These are exactly the times when meditation is needed the most. It never fails. Inertia comes in and makes us feel that we don't want to, but, if we can use our will at just those times, we will start to overcome our patterns of laziness and putting things off. What we are doing at these times is identifying with our negative habits instead of with the joy that comes when we do the work.

If we do stop meditating we soon start to feel like we are slipping back into the old ways and have to make what seems like incredible amounts of effort to pull ourself up again by our own bootstraps. Often we don't bother— but as the days roll by there's a nagging feeling that we are missing something.

Another pitfall is when we feel that meditation isn't working, that we are making no progress at all, or are falling asleep instead of meditating. These are common experiences and must not be identified as necessarily true. Internal energy works in subtle ways and has laws of its own. It may be building up momentum without our knowing it. Another instance is when we are riding high on the energy we've already built up and the results we do get seem inconsequential. The discipline starts to lag because we feel, "Oh, I'm already high, I can skip this time." The times we think we can skip may be just the time when the energy is about to take us to our next step. If we stop for any of these reasons we've hit the snag, and before we know it we've slid. Either we will pull ourself up by our own bootstraps again and again until we see how it works and don't lag anymore no matter what happens, or we will give up in self-disgust. But here again, we've tasted the fruit and a nagging feeling from our Real Self comes to prod us.

With determined perseverance the effort eventually becomes effortless, just as eating or brushing our teeth is effortless. We learn how the energy flows. After a time the exercises and ritual of meditation are no longer needed as tools for growth. They become part of us and we use them at all times. In whatever we do there is meditation in action. But we must be careful not to deceive ourselves that we are already there. This is a new evolutionary step for us and we must begin at the beginning.

GROWING UP MEDITATING

From the day a child is born he is influenced continuously by the environment. Who knows what effects our mother's attitudes and colorings of consciousness had on us as newborns, or even in the womb? In our infant openness we receive our mother's and father's thoughts and feelings telepathically, as if by osmosis, and these impressions begin gradually to color our own view of the world. As we grow we become aware of brothers, sisters, friends, culture, society, school, teachers, TV, radio, news, etc. All of this input affects our consciousness. We reject some of it, we repress some of it, we identify with some of it or we accept some of it, depending on whether it gives us pain or pleasure, security or insecurity. And so our ego, our separate sense of I, our personality gets built. We lose contact with the pure consciousness with which we came to earth.

"Ego" is a widely used word these days, but it is not very well understood. Actually ego is the conglomeration of filters which we build up from the time we are born. As these filters build up we identify with them, thinking, That is me, that is what and who I am. When we ask most people, little and big, "Who are you really?" they say, "I'm me, I'm my body, me," and point to their body. But this is a false idea.

It's as if an angel who is one with the whole universe came to earth and tried on the suit of clothes of a prisoner in jail and then began to think, "I am a prisoner," and began acting like a prisoner, completely forgetting he is an angel. The ego is just the shadow of the Real Self. It is the Real Self identifying itself as my body, my emotions and my mind. Billions of human egos act like corked bottles floating in the ocean, separating themselves from the ocean, saying I am here and you are over there.

The more strongly we are identified with our ego as ourself, the more we won't want to get rid of it. It would be like destroying ourself. We've built it up and we are proud of it. But, in reality getting rid of it is only destroying the false image of who we think we are, so we can wake up to our true individuality. The true individual is not the egotist, but is ego-less, one with all. The word "individual" means indivisible, that which cannot be divided, the whole.

Why do we build up egos at all if we are just going to have to get rid of them? So we can become masters. Only then can we go beyond ego. Ego will lead us up and down and all around through pleasures and pains until we learn how it works and can tell real truth from false truth. Then we become a living master, having mastered the art of living.

A child who meditates correctly every day keeps some contact with the Real Self inside that is never conditioned by what happens, that is always pure. He is not as influenced. This does not mean that he is insensitive or closed to other people; it just means that he doesn't have to look outside himself so much for authority, security and confirmation. He has his own direct contact with inspiration and bliss and does not need to depend so much on all the external stimulation that bombards children. There is an inner resource that helps him make wise decisions and choices. This foundation of being in contact with his True Self keeps him clear. He will still experience impressions and input from others, but being strong in his center, much of it will just pass right through without conditioning his awareness and coloring his view of reality with cloudy filters. The younger the child is when he begins to properly meditate the easier it will be to stay clear.

As a child learns to meditate he develops another important tool— concentration. Concentration is the ability to focus the attention on any one thing for a period of time. In meditation the attention is focused on the deepest Self within, the Center. Let's imagine the wandering attention is like a negative electrical current and the Center positive. When, through concentrating, this negative current is joined with the positive Center— we connect— and a flow of energy, a flow of awareness occurs. The discipline of teaching a child to concentrate in meditation and go deep into that Center to experience the flow will result in definite, visible effects on his personality and in his activities. As he develops an overall ability to concentrate, whatever he does is better performed. Whatever problem he focuses his attention on he is able to extract greater wisdom from it. The deeply meditating child, when supported by a loving family life, can cut through obvious and subtle distractions and problems that other children get hung up in. For hyperactive, retarded or disabled children, meditation can offer new possibilities for development. It can do the same for the average or mentally gifted child. New areas of the brain are opened that few people have awakened.

Results can come very quickly for children. They have much less to undo than adults. Meditation is such a new thing in the West, and meditation for children is almost unheard of because it requires special effort on the part of adults, and most meditating adults have been too busy learning themselves. Bringing meditation to children is a way of preventing many emotional disturbances from forming as well as curing many that do arise. Of course meditation is not the only necessary ingredient, an understanding family environment is also essential. However, it may be the missing ingredient for many children. If you really want more contact and love with your children, and a closer family life, start meditating together.

Most parents, teachers and counselors in child care fields

don't yet have a glimmer of awareness that they are missing out on one of the most valuable methods to improve psychological health in a child. While watching a group of six-year-old youngsters grow in a meditation class we see wonderful things happen. One non-meditating mother commented, "I don't know if it's due to meditation or what, but my son's concentration span has doubled since he started coming to this class. You can see it in everything he does and it's making a difference at school." This child was considered to be hyperactive and had been attending a two-hour session of meditation and awareness games every Sunday for eight weeks. Another mother commented on how much calmer her child was, and how much happier she seemed with herself. And one mother mentioned that her child was showing much more consideration for other people's feelings. Just that opportunity to get very quiet, to get in touch with herself and be able to express her inner feelings and share with other children in expressing theirs, made her more aware of others' inner worlds. These are just a few examples. Results may not always be obvious right away. They can be very subtle. Often they crop up seemingly all of a sudden, like a new plant breaking through the earth.

For children of all ages, as well as for adults, it is important that the energy received in the Centering meditations be directed in activity to ground the current and for balanced development. The techniques given in this book are for a balanced growth in ordinary, everyday living.

THE ULTIMATE GOAL

The ultimate goal of meditation is to become totally open to the evolutionary unfoldment process in ourself. As we experience unfoldment within we begin to see unfoldment in the world around us. What we called "the mirror effect" cannot be too strongly emphasized. It is an important key. We will notice ourself reflected back more and more as we grow. Flashes of insight will come to reveal that there is *no real separation* between ourself and others. Any extraordinary or mystical experiences we may have must be considered as effects of this process of really waking ourself up to its true nature. Miracles, psychic experiences, visions, etc., are all part of the unfoldment. But to concentrate on any of these as a goal or an end in itself is sidetracking from the real goal of Oneness. In Oneness religious teachings like "The Lord our God is One," "I and My Father are One," "Before Abraham was I Am" and "I am that I Am" make sense and become personally applicable to us.

In the past, many people who have glimpsed the spiritual potential of man and decided to develop it have left the worldly life and gone into some monastic order. More recently many have found a teacher or guru with teachings on how to get to the pure state while still involved with the world and its problems. All of mankind is confronted today with the challenge to consciously evolve or be buried in a sea of insurmountable economic, political and social difficulties, built from humanity's collective filters. These difficulties are all effects of man's ignorance of his own Self. Solutions that are practicable for individuals living in present day society are required.

For those who have the drive to achieve full liberation it is best to find a teacher who has already evolved to the enlightened state and who has a complete course of study for your direct evolution. The question often arises, "Why can't I just do it myself?" The answer is simple but our stubborn personalities often don't want to hear it and block our progress. A teacher who has cleared his own way can help us see through our own darkness much more quickly. Without a teacher and techniques that have proven successful it is like grasping in the dark. We might find the light switch, but it may take a long time.

Just as we have to commit ourselves in order to make any love affair successful, so we have to make a commitment, with our Self, to make our individual love affair with the One a success.

Chapter 3

Meditation as a Family Affair

What we are really trying to do in this book is to acquire a new view of people, of all ages, from the inside-out. In order to fully understand how to bring meditation and awareness expansion to children, adults need to have more knowledge about how our own awareness operates, especially with children. So our exploration in these first few chapters is like looking through the eye of a camera taking a movie of some of the thoughts and feelings that go on inside the inner worlds of human beings. As we do this exploring we can find out about ourself in a totally new way.

Through our zoom lens we discover that humans do not know themselves and do not perceive crystal clear at all. The personal ego and its acquired filters always seem to get in the way of pure perception. We don't label this fact good or bad, right or wrong. It's just the way things are. The human predicament will remain in this semi-aware state until man decides to change it through mastering his own ego, the little personal self.

GETTING CLEAR AND STAYING CLEAR

Getting clear is the process of ego mastery and our ability to stay clear is the proof that we are succeeding. How can we use our present living situation, our family life, for getting clear and staying clear? First, we have to accept that our family situation, whatever it may be, is for our growth. Wherever we find ouself, it is because some part of our own consciousness has brought us there and is keeping us there. We have attracted our circumstances like a magnet attracts iron, through our own conscious and unconscious desires, guilts, fears, habits and beliefs. Those who have attained higher levels of awareness through self-mastery of the ego have all said the same thing, that somewhere hidden in the recesses of our unconscious self are the causes for every situation. These causes act as vibrating internal energy currents that work to create and attract our life situation whether joy-filled or pain-filled. To see how these currents work in ourself requires a lot of awareness and self-analysis. So we learn to use our living situation as a mirror

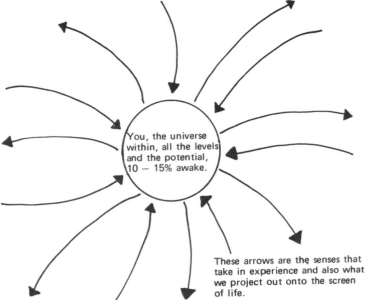

You, the universe within, all the levels and the potential, 10 — 15% awake.

These arrows are the senses that take in experience and also what we project out onto the screen of life.

for seeing into our own nature. Everything we experience is colored by the consciousness within us. All that we see on the movie screen of life mirrors our own consciousness back to us so we can discover ourself in it. Life is like a gigantic television program we're involved in right now. We don't need to be constantly drugged in our living rooms with the opiate of our TV set when we can learn how to live life fully. We have to learn to become aware of our reactions to others and why we act the way we do. As we come to know ourself we purify the consciousness and then we get a clearer life reflection back.

Since only ten to fifteen percent of our brain cells are functioning we can only experience a limited ten to fifteen percent of what's really going on in the universe. If one hundred percent of our brain potential was realized our experience of the universe would be totally different.

The pains and jolts life gives us purify and challenge us to wake up to more of our potential. If we can learn to use our pains as lessons to grow by we will convert them into joys and blessings. How can we learn to extract the most from our life? The family scene, where the drama of relationships is most intense, is where we must really face our identifications, projections and basic assumptions, to transform them into expanded awareness. It is the stage where behavior patterns are strongly programmed and acted out. The family— mother, father and children— or those people who live together and consider themselves as family, is the most vital situation for evolutionary transformation.

By learning to use family relationships as feedback to discover each other's projections, identifications and basic assumptions, we get clear. When we live closely together we are continuously absorbing thoughts and feelings from each other. This is normal and natural since consciousness is not confined just to our bodies, but interacts with other consciousnesses around us. We have all had experiences of picking up the thoughts, feelings or attitudes of another. We don't usually think much of it when it happens. It seems natural and our minds are usually busy with our own little worlds. But, it is through deepening our awareness of what goes on in the inner worlds of others and what gets transferred to us, that we expand beyond the personality into Universal Consciousness, the goal of meditation. In order to do this we must become very aware of others, while at the same time remaining in contact with our own Center so we don't get pulled into their trip. Practicing this awareness stretches our consciousness beyond its ego bounds. When we can experience the inner worlds of flowers, trees, stars, animals and people, we are expanding the little self to the cosmic Self.

We begin to realize that to really get clear of ego obstructions and stay clear, we will have to view our being human in an entirely new light. Evolution has been going on for millions of years, yet mankind is just beginning (in the past one hundred years) to wake up to the fact that evolution is going on. Of course there have always been exceptional individuals, especially in the East who have been aware of this fact Only in the past twenty years has there been a movement of large numbers of individuals who are waking up to the realization that they can do something to consciously enhance their own evolution. The revelation that humanity as a whole group must move into a new level of awareness or risk destroying itself is now dawning in the minds of many. The discovery of the tremendous power latent in the invisible atom is occurring simultaneously with the discovery of the tremendous power latent in the invisible soul. The nucleus of the atom contains the intelligence programming for the atom. The nucleus of man's soul, his spiritual center, contains the intelligence programming for man, which man can learn to tap. The nuclear energy potential in both atom and man has barely been demonstrated, but one thing is certain: either mankind learns to use the consciousness and energy constructively for nuclear evolution or we risk nuclear destruction. The decisions are up to man, for the intelligence programming has given him free will to choose. Nuclear evolution begins, not with atomic laboratories, but with contacting the nuclear Self within us to generate our own nuclear energy, which can move mountains and change our life.

As children and adults, we are all the time "psyching out" our family situation, seeing what we can do, what we can't do, what will bring a happy response and what will bring an angry response. Since it is the things that bother us that we have the most to learn from, it is important to discover how to deal with them in an evolutionary way. Every time we find ourself involved in an argument or disagreement, we must learn to ask ourself, "What am I really feeling? Am I really listening to the other? Am I expressing my true feelings or am I just using words that don't say enough? Am I or the other assuming something that isn't true? Do we have some false expectations of each other?" If we are being disturbed by someone we must discover what assumptions we are holding on to that lets us get disturbed. The examples of Jim and John and Bob in Chapter Two illustrate this need. Similar situations occur between parent and child.

For example, Mother is disturbed that six-year-old Susy can't read the first grade reader and other classmates, many from less educated backgrounds, can. Mother worries it is a reflection of her. She has tried to give Susy the best headstart and Susy just isn't doing well in reading. In a moment of frustration she tells Susy she is being lazy and not trying. Susy is deeply hurt, feels Mother doesn't love her. Mother doesn't realize that her *assumption* is that Susy can move faster. Susy might be a slow reader until age eight or ten and then pick up. There may be many reasons that Susy is slow, including physical eye development. Mother is so caught up in herself and her own self-respect that she does not really get into Susy's world and discover her needs. The effort to probe the causes of disturbances and frustrations in ourself first, then in others and in our children is the basic clearing exercise, to go beyond our filter mirrors. It requires much skillful practice. In other words, we learn to point the finger at ourself before pointing it out toward anyone else. And, we must teach our children this discipline as well. They need to look at their own faults before blaming other people.

Children who are taught meditation and awareness expansion experience an inner balance between what goes on in their inside, feeling world and the outside world of life around them. They are able to experience their own and other's inner worlds with understanding rather than accusing others of being wrong, or feeling that they are always being put down. This harmonizing of the inner life and the outer life leads to unity and oneness. These children gain strength and sureness that they take with them and build upon throughout life. Learning to be clear and stay clear brings the child a strong sense of social responsibility as he learns to extend his clear seeing to larger social problems as well. He gains the ability to condition his own life and help society through mastering his inner world of energies— thoughts, feelings, images. This is real freedom.

DEEPER SHARING AND DEEPER LOVE

In order to gain a deep understanding about meditation with children and families, we need to have some understanding about love. Love is the true motivating force behind family relationships. The cosmic evolution of intelligence is also an evolution of love. Love and intelligence are intertwined, not separate, and act through all of nature, in the ants, flowers, birds, bees, stars. Wherever we look we can experience them. Life is mating everywhere, in fantastically intricate patterns and cycles. Atoms unite to form molecules, molecules unite to form cells, cells unite to form organs, organs unite to form bodies, always expressing a more cooperative, higher form of life. As the family lives, grows and works together, love and intelligent response to life can be nurtured. But the opportunity is stifled in most families. Too many unsolved problems create the high rate of divorce and separation and bring turmoil and distress. As in a cancerous organ, divisiveness sets in between the cells until the life is destroyed.

The family bonds that used to give sustaining purpose to the family, in spite of problems, are gone. Traditionally, the family bonds have been held together by economic, social and religious customs. Now, all of these traditions are being challenged. When we live with another for awhile we develop emotional dependencies and we feed off them. Sometimes couples stay together just to maintain their emotional security, or for the sake of the children, even when there is little growth, real communication or fulfillment in their relationship. But what kind of love is this? When there is lack of growth there can be no real fulfilling love so the consciousness quickly goes to wallow in problems, live in the past, or look for diversions as an escape. We often try to keep up with the Joneses or run constantly to movies, parties and restaurants, to distract ourselves from our stale, unfulfilling lives with each other. It seems so normal and becomes such a pattern that we don't even realize we are compensating for not facing ourselves and our need for a living love. We assume that our life is the normal way people live.

With birth control available marriage itself has been challenged. More open attitudes regarding sex have developed. A recent national scholastic poll among teenagers in school showed that forty percent didn't even feel marriage to be important. Another factor, the rise of religious doubt, has left a spiritual void in many families. The result of these and many more economic and social changes has placed marriage on very shaky grounds. Falling in love, the need for a companion, children and security are the main factors that keep people getting married. But they are not enough for people to stay married. The divorce rate, now at thirty to fifty percent in the U.S. is still rising, whereas twenty-five years ago, divorce was hardly considered socially acceptable. What is needed for real fulfillment are new evolving values and lifestyles that will fill the void left by the cracking of the old traditions that have previously held marriage and family together.

There is a reluctance to replace old traditions with uncertain new ones that may be no more fulfilling than the old ones. And, while the shortcomings of the old traditions are generally seen, the real needs of man are not so clear. The new way that will finally replace the old is going to have to be based on an evolutionary value system, one that is vibrant, alive, and can move with the changing needs of man. An evolutionary system is tuned to the evolutionary intelligence that can only be contacted by going to the nuclear center and expanding our consciousness. Without this attunement man's values stay limited to his own beliefs. Man's beliefs are products of his own level of awareness and mind traps. Man tries to hold on to his beliefs for security, even when they no longer meet his real needs. They get fixed and then often have to be changed by disruption and revolution. But most revolutions just set up new belief systems and don't get to the real needs of the individuals involved. An evolutionary values system foresees that there always will be change, and real security can only be found when we make growth and change itself our security, our way of life. Growth and changing together is living love. Love and commitment in marriage are alive and growing when they are based on this evolutionary attitude—more than they can ever be when bound by social or religious dogma.

The idea of evolutionary growth and change as the key to fulfilling love is not understood or recognized by most people. But the children of today and the young adults, who are inheriting a world of instability and changes, know that a new way must be evolved.

Something has to be felt as lacking to make people want to delve deeply into spiritual and psychological growth. This growth helps to release being dependent on others and insecure, which blocks pure love. Most people just keep on the way they are. They busy themselves with work, hobbies, babies and diversions, pushing their problems under the carpet so there is very little self-inquiry or soul-searching unless or until life deals them some painful traumatic experience that wakes them up to look within.

To see the cosmic purpose of marriage and family as a chance to work consciously together on evolutionary growth is a revolution in thinking for humanity. It has only been made possible by the scientific advances that have given man the potential for more freedom. There is more free time now for recreation, and birth control limits family size. Recreation means re-creation, and the family need now is to find fulfilling new ways to use its time and re-create itself, its true New Age function.

There are several stages which are important for us to trace in the evolutionary growth of the family if we are to see our present situation clearly. The first stage is where life just goes on, and we are not aware there is anything more for us than what we are doing. We go about our business, build patterns of relating to each other and avoid working through to a real union. We do not see that there is any better way to go. Then there's a stage where we have a great need for some deep fulfillment that will go right to the innermost core of being. We might have experienced an altered state of consciousness through a psychedelic experience, through meditation, or we may have read a book like this one. Something opens up. Then the stage of whether or not we are going to commit ourselves to the labor of love of seriously working on ourselves comes. We see that spiritual and psychological growth requires persistent work. Some of us realize it is the most rewarding work possible. But how many will accept the challenge and the changes it will bring? The decision is whether we want to commit ourselves to doing this deep work together and risk the unknown, to experience the fulfillment of discovering the True Self in the other. The commitment to discovering ourself in another is the commitment to true union with the other, and true selfless love. In this commitment we leave each person in freedom to be themselves, for the union is not based on personal attachment. Personal attachments create expectations, jealousies, and resentment, which constrict love, creating more filters and causing most of the problems in marriages. In being willing to release our at-

tachments we risk the unknown. But we have to be willing
to let go in order to reach the goal of pure love. Pure love is
the ultimate evolutionary soul purpose of marriage— to
discover the One in each other. Most people stay on steps
one or two which means we do not become aware of our
patterns or how they affect our relationships with family
and friends. From the time of youth, through marriage, to
the golden anniversary, most of us live off personal attachments and roles, and do not really know our own inner
being or the inner being of our husband or wife. It is going
to be up to the forward-looking adults and our children to
inaugurate the true evolutionary way of life.

How do we really go about learning to experience the
inner beings of others? First we have to establish a new
level of trust with each other. This trust comes through
forming a new family bond that is committed to openness,
to communing and to exploring life together. To make the
change to an evolutionary family takes a real knowing that
"I have had enough of the old ways." If only one spouse is
willing to change then the other will be left behind and there
will be a gap between them. By gently exploring meditation
and awareness expansion together we take our first real
steps into this unfamiliar territory. Children can only enter
into a conscious evolutionary family experience if the parents do. Parents always want their children to improve and
be the best, but how many parents will take the time to
work with their kids to improve themselves too? If we really want more love and to give our children more love we
will be willing to join them in growing.

THE EVOLUTIONARY FAMILY EXPERIENCE

We begin our evolutionary family life by first introducing
meditation into our family experience. The parents can
begin meditating first to gain familiarity with the process,
and then bring the children into their communion.
Everyone has heard the old saying that a family that prays
together stays together. True prayer touches the one

Center of life within each person, and this deep communing fuses the family group together at a very deep level of Being. But prayer is not as directed toward contacting the spiritual Center in oneself, unless we have learned to pray very deeply. Meditation is an ideal accompaniment to prayer in its ability to contact the Source quickly through relaxation, concentration and mind training. The One Source of Love and Life then becomes the Center of family life in a family that meditates together. Each member taps and shares fresh energy, love and inspiration during the family group meditations.

Meditating Family

Center

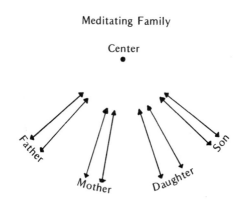

Non-meditating Family with no spiritual center, looks outwards for energy and stimulus

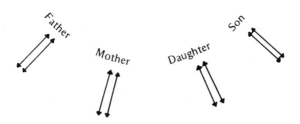

By creating an inner spiritual center in the family, a sustaining, building environment for each person's growth is provided. In meditation this inner center is based on the direct personal contact with pure energy and spiritual awareness, rather than on religion.

The Master and the scriptures are guides to how we can directly experience energy and pure consciousness for ourself. They are not substitutes for making our own direct contact which would deprive us from real spiritual fulfillment. This is one of the reasons religious traditions are declining today. The attempt to make the religion itself the Spiritual Center, rather than direct contact with Spirit, will not work. The true Spiritual Center brings open truth and intelligent examination of spiritual teachings for ourself, instead of blind acceptance of dogma. Blind acceptance is stifling to the truth-seeking quality of the human Spirit and is often rejected by aware young people. Through meditation a family can commune at home every day. For more fellowship we can get together to commune with other families or couples. Spirit cannot be confined to a church. Meditation as a scientific and psychological technique for increased energy, brain capacity and attuning to higher intelligence will dissolve the old separation of church and state because it goes beyond religious beliefs which often conflict. It is the essence of all religions stripped of their differences.

The silent meditation period is only half the work for the evolutionary family experience. Awareness exercises as active meditation are also needed to break down the barriers that separate us from each other. There are many meditation groups and teachings available today which neglect the work on the ego. Discovering our motives for our thoughts and actions is essential for enlightenment.

To make the most of the awareness exercises given here, we must really be open about our feelings. Achieving total openness in a family will be slow since we are not used to being truly honest even with ourself, let alone with someone else. Being closed begins when we are very little by what we feel we can and cannot share with our parents. When parents are not very honest about their own feelings with themselves or with each other, children become psychically aware of this block, and are unlikely to have the trust to share their inner worlds openly either. Many people believe they are open, but most of us have many inner feelings that never get expressed. The most tender moments between a man and a woman, between parent and child and between all people come when there is real sharing of feelings. This reflects trust.

Trust is a big thing in a family, from parent to child, from child to parent, from parent to parent, and child to child. Some children stop playing horsie, or acting out their fantasies as soon as someone else walks in the room, because they feel others do not share that reality. Grownups or even brothers or sisters might put down or negate that part of themselves. So, these children feel they cannot share their fantasies with the family. There is a fear they might be rejected in some way. It is rude for another family member not to respect children who need privacy. When privacy is intruded upon, feelings are run over roughshod and defenses get built internally in children to prevent anyone from getting inside. Defenses add to the lack of trust. "They can come interrupt my playing, but they aren't going to know what I'm really thinking and feeling inside." Invasion of privacy is due to lack of sensitivity or consideration for the child's world. Often the adult's internal judgment about what the child is doing is picked up by the child and makes him feel more separated and defensive. The way to dissolve these barriers and build trust comes by sharing activities together on levels meaningful to the child, and by respecting and finding out what he is feeling. Playing make-believe together will encourage the child to open up with his dreams and fantasies. Learning to develop extrasensory perception together will encourage the child's natural development of intuition. Intuition is often easier for children to contact than adults, but because it is not encouraged it does not develop. Doing some simple gestalt dream analysis together, discussing the most pleasurable and most painful events of the past day or week or year are some of the ways to promote healthy openness. The exercises in Chapter 7 are designed to develop sharing on all the seven levels of awareness.

Can you really be open about nitty-gritty feelings with those with whom you live? Are you afraid they will think less of you if you do? Would they react and make you feel put down in some way? Do you filter a lot of your deep feelings when you speak with others and therefore lose contact with these feelings yourself? Can those you love be open with you? Or do they fear your rejection, criticism or denial? Stop for awhile and ask yourself each of these questions. Find out what really is happening in your family situation. Then you will know what you need to work on the most.

SOLVING FAMILY PROBLEMS

The first step in breaking through our blocks in the evolutionary family experience is to admit we do not know ourself or our children very well. Then we have to make the commitment to do the exercises that lead the family from the old ways into the new and be open to the changing process. We have to muster our courage and be willing to challenge family members on their attitudes and assumptions in a loving way, and be ready to be challenged by them. Only than can we probe our patterns and problems and get to real honesty and integrity. Young children must be included in this work as much as possible as part of the family. They will grow up with it, learning to be open as much by the atmosphere as by participation— in the same way as they would learn to be closed.

We call this way of handling problems *creative* conflict. Conflict is not rejected as bad or unspiritual. Instead it is used constructively and creatively for growth. We need to transform the hurtful and destructive type of conflict that often occurs. In creative conflict we agree to disagree and to respect each other's right to disagree. We explore together our real causes for disagreement through sharing with the other real life examples of how we feel about what we see them do.

Learning how to get in touch with feelings and express them to each other is only part of openness. We also need to learn how to get out of our self and be able to really experience the nature of the problem in the other without judging or filtering. We can only do this by listening, receiving and being open to their inner world. These qualities of receptivity have to be cultivated. Once openness is established with one person it gives us the courage to carry it into other relationships— with friends, teachers and co-workers. Often we feel, as children and as adults, that we can be more open with someone outside the family. We want to have a close confidant. Increasingly people seek out psychologists òr psychiatrists to fill this role, so they can have their need to empty and share real feelings and get honest feedback fulfilled. Too often feelings and problems just get muddied at home and get buried. Real feelings generally remain unexplored or even unknown to us until we can talk about them to a receptive confidant who we trust won't react against us.

Most parents really want their children to feel they can trust and confide in them. But in spite of their good intentions, most parents react negatively to their children when they do confide, and put their own trip on them in the name of guidance. Those children who don't have enough guidance or limits to control them become just as unstable and confused as children who have been suppressed by too much authority. When authority is enforced along with understanding of the child's feelings and needs, it is balanced and in tune with nature. Then children will spontaneously follow; they won't be squelched. Often older children reject many of their parents' feelings, values and authority which makes communication near to impossible. When the parent tries to conquer these differences with an authority trip saying, "My way is right, and as long as you live under my roof you'll do things my way," without explaining why he feels the way he does as well as finding out why the child feels the way he does, he will completely cut off the channel for openness. The authority alone will prevail and the real feelings and reasons for them will be buried and never shared in understanding. Then resentment and rebellion are bound to set in.

Many adults and children are very stubborn and refuse to look inside themselves or into each other. Some refuse to change even though they say they are willing to. Children often pick up these attitudes from a parent, so the parent is just getting himself back through his child's attitude. In an evolutionary family the stubbornness must be pointed out and worn away if there is to be any real growth. Awareness exercises show us how to do this.

As we probe into our family relationships we discover that children present wonderful mirrors for parents to see themselves. Let's look at a typical example. Mother says to three-year-old Alice, "No you may not do that. Don't do that." Alice runs off crying into her room and grabs her stuffed doll. Her feelings are hurt. Lately Alice has been doing this when Mother says no. She never used to react that way. She used to listen to Mother's reasons and accept them. It is a new pattern.

Mother, who is a meditator, feels Alice is experiencing a new sense of separation from her which is part of attaining her own identity. So Alice reacts emotionally when told no because she feels Mother is separating herself from her. Now this reaction is common for children Alice's age. But Mother wants to know if there is more involved. Does it have something to do with starting nursery school and being told no by a teacher? Mother looks inside her own life and admits to herself that she gets quite emotionally upset inside when her husband and other people chastise her for some misaction. She reacts personally by feeling very hurt. So now she thinks, "I'm so surprised that this pattern is occurring already in my three year old. Did she pick it up from me? Is it natural? I don't feel I am projecting on her, I'm just saying no as mother authority; that what she is doing is not to be done. But she takes it as a personal offense all of a sudden. Is there a different way to handle the situation so the light of truth can enter in?''

Let's look deeper at Mother. Perhaps Mother's emotional reaction to authority makes her own authority come across too strong, so she creates the same response in Alice and maybe in others too, like a chain reaction. Perhaps Alice is starting to feel how much Mother dislikes authority laid on her and here Mother is giving her the same treatment she dislikes. So Mother must not like her or she wouldn't do something to her that she doesn't like herself. What about Dad? Dad is also very sensitive to any kind of assertiveness by Mother. During a deep conversation Mother says to Dad, "I don't feel like you are really listening to me. I'm trying to explain my feelings to you and you're off in your own mind comparing my feelings with your friend Chuck's the other day. You're not really listening to me." Her tone is somewhat sharp and frustrated. Dad gets angry and frustrated too. He takes all assertiveness on his wife's part as a negative put down. So Alice may also be identifying with Dad, giving her all the more reason to take Mother's assertiveness toward her personally.

Now, of course, all of this is unconscious in Alice and the reasons are unconscious to Mother and Dad as well, until they look into them. Husband and wife develop ego ways of relating to each other which develop into strong attitudes. Children pick these attitudes up, absorb them and react to them.

What can Mother do? Mother can try to help Alice by waiting until she calms down and then letting her know that she is with her, that she understands how she feels. The vibes of Mother's caring and understanding are important even though Alice may continue to be upset and is too young to be able to understand Mother's reasoning. Mother decides, "If I'm clear about what I'm saying and my own motive behind it, I just have to go ahead, even if met by resistance. Nonetheless my efforts to acknowledge Alice's reality helps to build real trust between us."

What role should authority play in the family? Should Mother's authority always be supported unquestioningly by Dad? and vice versa? Or must the whole nature of authority be reconsidered? If the bond of trust is to be developed then the authority cannot be based on whim or parental compensation for some problem. But strong authority is also needed for children to develop a strong will for self-mastery and to sustain the deep sense of security with the parents that every child thrives on.

Let's look at another example: "Johnny, clean up your room. I've told you for the fourth time. I'm going to have to punish you if you don't listen to me. Now go and do it." Cleaning up their room is a hateful and boring chore for many kids. "I've got to do it, just because Mom said so," is often the feeling. The deepening love experience developed through meditation and openness can begin to transform the parent-child authority relationship. Through increased open sensitivity with each other, Mother becomes aware of her child's inner world before she makes demands, and her child experiences a deep friendship with Mother that self-motivates him to want to participate in the family chores.

Nagging makes children turn a deaf ear until the parent explodes. As a little girl I can remember I felt my mother mostly criticized me when she was at the point of being upset and emotional, or else she'd start complaining when we were involved in other activities, for example, when she was busy working in the kitchen and I was getting ready to do something, or busy doing something. Admittedly, I was very ego-sensitive, not wanting to hear her at all, or to feel there might be something wrong with me. I was afraid to be wrong so I learned to justify, rationalize or wiggle my way out of what was being said rather than really look at it. When a teacher or a friend, or sometimes even my brother told me something to improve on, it was easier to listen because it was given unemotionally and didn't feel like an

accusation. When advice or criticism was given emotionally, or when I was afraid I was being accused, I became
very resistant. Awareness exercises help root out these
kinds of ruts in family relating.

Sometimes one parent supports the other parent's reaction toward the child, just to reinforce the other's authority,
and then the child is made to feel in the wrong, even though
he may have a very valid reason for feeling the way he does.

The Milk Episode: Alice has had a glass of milk and
asks for more. Mother pours another half glass. She drinks
that down and asks for more. Mother says, "No, you've
had enough." Alice says, "No, I haven't had enough."
Mother says, "Yes, I said you have. That's plenty." Dad
hears the conversation and says, "Alice says she hasn't had
enough. How can you say she has?" Dad identifies with
Alice this time instead of siding with Mother's authority.
Now Mother wonders what was the right thing in the situation. Did she have enough or didn't she? According to my
authority or hers? Then Mother starts to feel confused
about it all.

Mother and Dad start talking to try to sort out what's
best and Alice watches them feeling, well Dad is on my
side, and she wonders what will happen. They talk, but it
doesn't get resolved. Mother ends up frustrated, exasper-
ated, feeling Dad should have supported her and Dad ends
up wondering why Mother wouldn't believe Alice. Maybe
she really needed the extra nutrition. They all three leave
the table wondering. Alice forgets the incident quickly as
she goes to play with some clay. But does she forget? Or
does it become part of her? She may be feeling Dad's for
her and Mother's against her and that is why she gets hurt
so much now when Mother challenges Alice's authority,
saying, "No, you may not do that." Alice senses a conflict
regarding authority between her parents and expresses it by
rejecting Mother's authority with hurt and tears.

What can we do with this milk situation? This kind of
episode occurs daily in many families in many different
ways. The way we can probe deeper is to discover motives.

What was Mother's real motive in saying, "No, you have had enough milk?" Is it that milk costs seventy cents a half-gallon and money is low, so Mother feels she's had enough because it costs so much? Alice doesn't know that. And Dad may not have thought of that. When Mother says "you've had enough," Alice may still be really thirsty and might quite honestly respond, "No, I haven't had enough." If Mother insists, then she is denying Alice's reality and they are not really communicating. Mother has just asserted her authority and not explained why even to herself. If she had, she might have decided powdered milk could be made or have offered Alice juice or water instead. In this case Mother's authority comes across as a denial of Alice's need and is not based on understanding.

To just assert authority on a child, without conveying why, just because it's Mother who said so, does not promote trust and understanding. Dad reacted and sensed Alice's feelings shouldn't just be denied like that. But, he reacted to Mother and wasn't able to explain himself either. All three get emotionally involved and have strong feelings, but none can see the situation clearly.

As observers, with zoom camera lenses, we can see into the motives, but the test for each of us is, how do we improve our own involved situations. Every family has to cope with similar situations and no one wants to belabor every single point out of fear of, Am I right? Am I wrong? Life would lose its joy and spontaneity. Sometimes it is easy to recognize the need to improve our communication, but it is often difficult to build up the desire to bring about a true change or get some help. It's easier to stick to the old ways and patterns. Most of us are very resistant to changing our behavior. So we must provide techniques that will work to create the overall needed changes.

A young child learns to adjust to parents' behavior, but his inner being will build attitudes and react around them if his real self is denied in some way. If Dad keeps getting angry with him unjustly a child's sense of self-worth is damaged. On the other hand if Dad's anger is appropriate to the situation and not just based on his own problems, the child will gain in having to take responsibility for himself and in self-respect. Expressing feelings and honest emotion to a child, whether anger or affection, speaks true because it is real. The tremendous impressive influence of teachers on children's psycho-emotional states is similarly important.

The earlier we can give our children, teachers and parents tools to see themselves and others clearly, the more we will further human understanding. The earlier we can aid our children in developing their own hotline to pure consciousness through direct perception of the One, the less they will be influenced by adults' negative trips.

In addition to teaching children how to meditate and use awareness expanding games and exercises, we teach them how to redirect their energies and how to take responsibility for their own actions. When family squabbles arise, each family member learns to point the finger at himself *first*, and see how he may have been involved in creating the situation, rather than lashing out at the other. When Father yells at Junior for having left the cap off the bottle of glue for the third time, Junior will respect Father's feelings a lot more if he sees Father just as ruthless with himself. Often Father yells at Junior for not doing things that he himself doesn't do, like picking up clothes after himself, or giving moral advice that he doesn't follow himself. Such hypocrisy can eat at children, inside, until they learn how to sublimate it or shrug it off. Still, it has its effect.

When the parent-child relationship is built on a new base of openness and willingness to challenge our own assumptions and each others, in a spirit of love, then we begin to flower a new type of love in family living. Then problems are not buried, so no lurking poisonous monsters of hidden resentments can leap out to cause great pain. A new integrity is brought to the family which helps to eliminate the generation gap. The generation gap is mostly due to a lack of ability to understand each other's communication, not to a lack of talking. If children and adults have not gotten into each other's inner worlds while the child was growing up, then it is only natural that differences will accumulate and surface as the child becomes more independent. Our goal isn't to eliminate differences in thinking, but to add true understanding and acceptance of each other.

So here we are, wherever we are, in our family life, ready to begin a new kind of relating. We begin by learning to meditate and to meditate frequently alone and together. We also start to be more open with our real feelings, to challenge ourself on our motives and challenge each other, as best we can, with love, on our assumptions, projections and identification. In doing this we take fuller responsibility for our own and our family's psychological and spiritual health. We adults and children are shown how to become more responsible for our own use of consciousness. When we have seen the need to develop consciousness and solve family squabbles in a new, less authoritarian way, we bring parents and children together in a deeper bond of love and trust.

EXPLORING LIFE TOGETHER— EXERCISES FOR HONESTY AND OPENNESS

Learning how to use the power of the creative imagination is a very powerful tool for changing consciousness. But it has natural rules of operation which must be taught to children and adults in order to achieve good results. We all use our imagination unconsciously, from hopes and fantasies to fears that condition our lives, but we don't realize how much more we can use it consciously to recreate our life to what we want it to be.

To use the imagination well, we begin in the still space in meditation. In that space we get ourself out of the way and make room for fresh insights to come. Being in that still space is the time when the incoming energy can best be directed into new patterns. Whatever thoughts or desires we put into consciousness at the high point of our meditation will have a potent creative energy behind them. The Eastern meditators call this energy *kundalini*, we use "kundalini" to do everything— image, think, feel, and move but it is most potent when we are perfectly still in meditation. If we vividly image a more perfect relationship and keep imaging it, that high energy will be set in motion by the power of our directed image to manifest what we've imagined.

There is a spiritual law of consciousness that energy follows thought. It is because of this law that the power of positive thinking is such a popular, workable tool. If we put in a negative thought, or a doubt or fear, that will happen too, and short circuit our positive programming. So in this meditative state it is necessary to be careful to put in only the positive for ourself and others. If we program love or something helpful to another we will receive that back as well, like a mirror.

The energy also is powerful when we are highly emotionally charged, for example, a mother's ability to lift an automobile to free her child pinned beneath.

The awareness exercises are structured games for learning how to develop and direct consciousness, to be done alone and together. They should be carried out at a time mutually agreed upon. When feelings and ideas are explored in an organized way family members become more concentrated and willing to listen. They take challenges less personally than if we were to nag them or to challenge them at emotional times.

The most important thing needed for openness is for the child not to feel judged, for the parent to be able to set aside his own personal values and feelings to be able to really listen to the child. Then we can get deep inside where the child is coming from and not just assume that it is where we believe it is. Then the child will feel safe to expose himself and know it will be accepted.

With structured exercises it's easier to generate willingness to work on problems. The exercises given here are to increase openness in the family. They must be repeated frequently. The depth of open response will be proportional to the amount of trust that is present. Watch those thoughts that you decide not to say.

In all these exercises we must be careful not to let ourselves get distracted. Getting into conversations about anything that is not related to the exercise is considered a distraction and not relevant. So keep your concentration one-pointed and follow the instructions for best results.

Meditate together before doing these exercises.

a) Sit in a circle, on the floor if possible, wherever is most comfortable. Have each member of the family say in a few sentences what they feel each of the others thinks about them and how they think of themselves. Is it the same? Don't get into a discussion, just go around. If you have a tape recorder, record the exercise. When you are finished going around then you can add comments and insights. Now do the same thing again, this time going deeper into your feelings. Listen to the tape recorder the next day. Note how much more you hear from it, and how different it is than during the exercise itself.

b) Say one thing to each family member that you've wanted to say to them and never have. Usually we let a great deal pass which builds up inside about the other, never really feeling we have the right, safe opportunity to say it, or dismissing it as not really important. Now's the time. The statement can be as simple as I don't like the shoes you wear or the way you slouch and I wish you'd try to improve on it, to more nitty-gritty statements like I feel you hide the truth a lot and tell me only half the story. Statements are said in love. There is no discussion until *after* each person has said their piece. Then take one of the comments at a time and begin exploring it together openly. Ask both the one who made the comment and the one who it was directed to, how it made them feel to say it and to receive it. Try to get into the feelings and reactions of both.

Many children and adults will show initial shyness or embarrassment at opening up and expressing themselves. Gently encourage them, but let them be. Total openness is not going to occur immediately. We have to trust our new situation first. If the parents can begin to open, then the children will naturally follow. We can help each other by asking, "Is there something more behind what you just said?" The other person may say, "It's too personal; I don't want to say it." We can keep probing kindly, but we must respect this statement as the person's choice if they wish to stick to it. When children and adults finally can feel able to share the deeper feelings, fears, jealousies, thoughts, etc., it will be a great relief to them.

c) One person sits in the middle of the circle or, in the love seat, in turn. Each of the others sitting around the circle say one positive thing they really like about the person in the center and one thing they feel the person needs to improve or work on. No two people may say the same thing. Someone is the recorder and makes a chart like a grid of what is said and who said it.

Each person also makes statements about himself, so all the squares are filled. Each one says what he likes most about himself and what he needs to work on in himself. After the chart is complete there can be discussion about how the needed improvements can be worked on, but there should be no discussion during the exercise. The family can explore whether one person's suggestion for another is that person's problem too or whether it applies more to the other. Could it be a projection?

Sometimes one person will tell everyone pretty much the same thing. This is a good sign that what is said is mostly in the eye of the beholder, in the person who said it. Whatever disturbs you about anyone else is *your* problem too, if you're letting it bother you. This doesn't mean that the other may not have something to work on as well. We can use the other family members to help us see who has the real problems. Is it Mother's expectation of Susy that she should wear long hair and frilly clothes when Susy likes to climb trees, have cropped hair and wear jeans? Is Susy just being free and wanting to be like her brother? Or does Susy have a real problem? Other children in the family often have wonderful insights that can see into even very deep family problems if they are encouraged to meditate on them and bring out their conclusions. If the child on the love seat, or "hot" seat begins to feel upset or threatened and gentle encouragement doesn't work, then it's better to stop until another time.

At the beginning of the exercise, after the unifying meditation, children might need to be reminded that this is not a teasing game, but to put their whole heart into it. If any of the children begin teasing or acting disruptive they can be excused from the room until they can cooperate. Young children should be included when they are able to participate, otherwise the exercise should be done when they are in bed or somewhere where Mother won't be distracted.

One important exercise that makes all the other family exercises work is what we call "mirroring." Mirroring develops proper listening and receptivity. Each person has to mirror back, in their own words, what the other person has just said to them. Other members look for bad listening. They listen to see if there are any filters, projections and assumptions in the feedback. Mirroring is of vital importance in the family to get true, clear communication. Throughout the book we have emphasized how the world mirrors or feeds back to us what is in our own consciousness and what we put out. The mirroring exercise helps us to realize how this works and how to use it as a tool for our growth. When we are close, as in a family, the projections and the assumptions and reactions come and go so fast that true uncolored listening rarely takes place. Our own thoughts spinning in our minds usually condition what we hear, and we don't hear what the other person means at all. The mirroring exercise is given on page 141.

Few families are aware of the evolutionary potential, the potential for much deeper love, perception and understanding, that comes through seeing each other as mirrors and reflectors by which we can learn more about ourselves. We are generally too busy blaming others, and not seeing ourself in them.

Any group can serve as a positive feedback once they know how. Groups of people can get together to compare notes on their growth work, brainstorm problems and get fresh mirroring. Inter-family group work is especially important for single parent families to get feedback and give each other support. Consciousness becomes intertwined.

Its positive side brings closeness, love and union. Its negative side is sharing others' delusions. Sometimes we might get insights into our family's group delusions by working with another family. As we eliminate the delusions we purify the love as well as our perceptions. If once every few weeks we share the problems that have arisen with another family, the objectivity of the other may help us come to a clearer understanding. Instead of getting together to play bridge or have dinner and gossip or talk about politics while the kids watch TV, we can get together to do some real work on ourselves by having a family nucleus session. Inter-family work is more exciting and meaningful than any card game. This evolutionary exploration can be coupled to family outings, camping trips and other things done together to add more depth to them.

Creative conflict, self-examination and spiritual growth will do more to bring peace to each man, woman and child's heart and peace to the world than any discussion of the world situation. There can never be peace in the world until there is true peace in the lives of the individual who make up the world. Compare this evolutionary approach to family life with your own childhood experience, where this kind of awareness was absent or pushed under the carpet or ended up in an argument that got nowhere. Remember how it felt for you as a child to experience this, and imagine yourself as a child having had the opportunity for the evolutionary experience we are talking about here.

As we explore life together in these new ways we learn to expand beyond the instinctual parent-child love. We also expand beyond the usual emotional attachments to a true sharing of pure love. This experience of love is rich and flowing. We learn to share love on all the seven levels of being so it is complete. Love deepens as our honesty, our openness, and our ability to listen to others' worlds deepens. Suddenly we find ourselves really communicating and communing. The play of love in nature begins to show itself all around us. We laugh and cry in joy. Lovers' quarrels are seen as frustrated attempts to communicate feelings to each other. As painful and ineffective as they usually are, we see them as a form of love, as the lowest form of human love. We always hurt and get hurt by the ones we love on the human level, because we have emotionally given each other the power to hurt by being attached. Our ability to trust suffers the more we are hurt. We can rebuild that trust when we can see and love the True Self acting through ourself and through our loved ones. Only then are we free of the attachments, the unconscious games and selfishness of the little self that have tossed us around.

Exploring life together with the goal of evolutionary unfoldment is a new social experience. As a way of life it minimizes the need for unnecessary material belongings because our fulfillment is not in them. Eliminating the control of money as the means of satisfaction in our lives is extremely important for spiritual fulfillment. It will become more important should we find ourselves in an economic depression. An evolutionary life can transform and expand normal family activities and supply a self-reliance in each person that will stand secure despite changes that may occur in the family, in society or in the world.

Chapter 4

How to Meditate with Children

FAMILY GROUP MEDITATIONS

Children rarely like to be told anything, especially if they fancy doing something else at the time. In teaching them how to meditate it is best to have a set time of day in which it is done as a family activity. Some children will reject it. They will find it strange, too different from what they are used to doing. Some children may reject meditating out of laziness or simple resistance to discipline, and some may show an unwilling stubbornness to do anything different. Most children, however, will want to do it most of the time and will not want to at other times. This response is normal, but they should be strongly encouraged to do it daily until it becomes a natural daily habit. Then they will look forward eagerly to it as a time when their deepest being is fulfilled and as a favorite family activity.

Whenever a child absolutely refuses to cooperate with the meditation or becomes disruptive, he needs to be given a firm choice. Either he may stay and get into the meditation or he may do something quiet away from everyone else. This time should be a time when he is to be with himself, and tempting alternatives like playing with a friend or watching cartoons should not be offered. We insist on children taking naps, brushing teeth or other rituals we feel are necessary for their health. A period of turning within each day to meditate is just as necessary for good psychological health. If something very important and exciting comes up just at the time for meditation, the family can decide whether to postpone the meditation until later, or to consider it the more important activity. It is not wise to constantly force a child to meditate. Whenever we force we have the dominating authority problem again of do it my way, regardless of how you feel. This domination always backfires into resentment. If the parents do it, if it is part of the family life, the children will accept it much more readily. Until meditation and awareness training becomes a common activity in schools, among friends and in the home, some children will resist at first and others will love it.

We must march through this early phase by setting the example and doing it regularly ourselves. Children, especially young children, will learn by imitation and identification with the parent. After some encouragement most will join in eventually of their own free will as they see those nearest to them become more involved. It is most rewarding when children participate and respond willingly. They feel they are taking responsibility for the family communion too.

Steady encouragement is essential because the attention span is short, and the typical "I don't feel like it today" will sometimes appear. Giving a balking child a choice between doing two things, when persuasion fails, allows them an essential freedom. Limiting the number of choices shows them clearly that there are limits in life, and maintains the true parental authority as a guide. Either you stop throwing those toys or you go sit in your room is a definite choice. So is either you brush your teeth every morning and evening or you will have cavities that the dentist will have to fill. And, so is either you meditate with us or you go look at a book quietly in your room. Children realize they have a decision to make and must take responsibility for their choice. Life teaches us all in the same way. How often do we adults say "Should I do this or that?" By giving us choices, life teaches us to think ahead to the consequences of our actions. What will the results be either way? This thinking builds our sense of responsibility as well as our foresight.

The regular daily family time for meditation can be extended to include an awareness exercise, sharing of feelings and ideas, or ironing out problems. All of these activities are helped if we meditate and get Centered first. Also, when big problems arise, stop everything and sit down to meditate. Each person will become calm and will be able to get in touch more deeply with what they are really feeling. A more difficult step to make is getting in touch with what the other person is feeling too. It may bring a creative solution to mind, and certainly will transmute the level of working on the problem to more total seeing. A Centering meditation can be done spontaneously at any time when the need is felt— before going to bed, before a test in school or before any difficult time.

When you have found the most convenient time for your daily meditations, try to keep it regular. Rhythmic regularity. is natural. When something interferes with. your schedule, use the next available time. Pick a quiet room where everyone can sit on chairs or pillows comfortably. Outdoors is a wonderful place to meditate provided insects and noises are not distracting. Begin by reading the instructions to all the family on how to prepare for meditation. If you have a tape recorder you can tape them ahead of time so that everyone can listen. All of the following instructions on how to meditate can be used when meditating by yourself too.

MEDITATION WITH THE VERY YOUNG— PRENATAL TO FIVE YEARS

Children of this age group are the most difficult to get to sit still, but there are ways. Sitting still is the first lesson for everyone so we must be able to sit still ourselves before showing our children how.

Expectant mothers who meditate often can feel the baby relax in the womb when they sit to meditate, or alternatively begin to kick and move. The baby responds to the energy coming in. Meditation can help the mother tune in to her unborn child and actually deeply sense the baby's vibration. Some meditating mothers are able to consciously commune with the soul before the birth. Expectant mothers can spend part of their meditation period each day meditating on the baby. Focus the attention on the baby and open to it by sending a wave of love. Do this by imagining the baby in your mind's eye and send love gently flowing into the baby. Then relax and be open to receive a vibration back. You may or may not feel a response. Keep it up and eventually you will feel your attunement deepening. The energy and love are carried on your thought waves to the baby whether or not you are sensitive to it. The child's body is part of your body and will automatically receive the soothing and harmonizing energies that you receive in meditation. You can chant the sound Aaahhh or Ooommm softly as you send your love out from the heart. Sound waves help to concentrate and carry vibration. Receive love back from the One in the stillness between each note. Listen in that stillness. As you meditate in this way you may have intuitive feelings about changes in diet or rest or other aspects of your life that will help the pregnancy. The ability to deeply relax which meditation brings will also make the labor and birth easier.

When the baby is born and for the first year, the mother (and father) should hold him or her for a short while in meditation every day, communing in the One. As soon as the baby is old enough, begin letting him or her sit next to you while meditating. Even when the exploring stage begins, a minute or two of silent meditation for the baby is usually possible. A few minutes will be about maximum for most children until around the age of three, unless the child has really learned how to go deep into himself. At age three you can encourage him to sit a little longer with an imaginative meditation, with chanting vibrating primal sounds like Aaahhh or Ooommm, or a simple meditation exercise that will engross his attention. Even a minute of meditation can bring Centering if there is real concentration.

For children three to five it is helpful to teach them how to Center in meditation and then give them some activity to do after the meditation that will teach them how to use and ground their energy. They will learn to go within, concentrate, then direct the energy outward, continuing to concentrate it into some challenging activity, like setting the table, feeding the cat a full bowl of milk or drawing. When there is a child in this age group in a family with older children he may not always be able to cooperate to the end of the family meditations. He should stay as long as he can and then should know to leave quietly for his room. If he is totally unable to participate he should be given some other quiet activity to do and told not to disturb. A meditation suited to three to five year olds should be done with him at another time.

Some children this age can join in a longer meditation, if they are very relaxed. It is important that children get as relaxed as possible before the meditation, especially if they have been doing something very active right before meditation time. Chanting primal sounds creates resonance, bringing a ringing, vibrating sensation into the head which feels different and good. This type of chanting mixed with meditation and a meditation prepared for them on tape that they can listen to with earphones will help keep their concentration going longer.

Some of the family awareness exercises will be easy enough for them to stay with, but for those which are too involved something else must be planned for them in advance. With a little forethought and preparation the needs of all family members of different ages can be met and the family meditation still occur regularly.

A MEDITATION EXERCISE FOR THREE TO FIVE YEAR OLDS

Use inflection and different tones to keep it interesting. Keep ahead of the child. Start with a few yoga exercises to relax and tune the body, for example, the Dog, the Shoulderstand, the Cobra, the Tree. (See Chapter 5.)

Let's sit up straight with our legs crossed and our hands palms up on our knees or thighs. Be sure to keep the back straight. Have you ever seen puppets on strings? Imagine there's a string on top of your head pulling you up so your spine is straight. Close the eyes. Now breathe in through

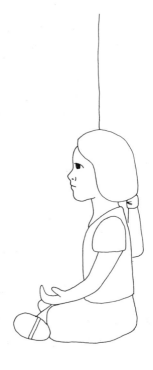

the nose slowly. Keep the mouth closed. Breath out through the nose. . . . Let's do this again. Breathe in as I count to three (1 . . . 2 . . . 3). Hold to three (1 . . . 2 . . . 3). Breathe out slowly through the nose to a count of three (1 . . .2 . . . 3). Let's do this again and again. (Repeat the 1 . . . 2 . . . 3 breathing three or four times.) Now just relax and breathe like you usually do. Be still. In . . . and . . . out . . . in . . . and . . . out . . . feel like you are a wave on the sea. Rising slowly . . . up . . . and . . . down . . . each time you breathe . . . in . . . and . . . out . . . feel like you are the sea. . . . (Rest quietly, everyone being the sea until the child starts to move or be restless.)

Then say: Now let's tense our whole body, make fists, tense all the muscles in your legs, and feet, arms, chest, don't forget your face. Tense your mouth and nose too. Now, still sitting up straight, let go. Let all the energy out, out, out until you are empty, relaxed, completely empty. Not a drop left. Now, still sitting up straight, (whisper) very quietly, we look inside our self behind our closed eyes. Look at a place right between your eyebrows inside your forehead. Look up a little and in. Feel like you are at the center of your Self. Deep in your heart. There is a shining light right inside you, right there. Be the light.

If the child is not quiet and relaxed after "being the sea" do the tensing and relaxing and then add: Each time you breathe in and out like a wave you will go deeper and deeper into meditation. I'll count waves and when I get to ten you will be a quiet wave and you will be the calm sea, and you will be deeply relaxed. (Count slowly following the child's breathing) 1 . . . 2 . . . 3 . . . 4 . . . 5 . . . 6 . . . 7 . . . 8 . . . 9 . . . 10 . . . There, you are the calm, quiet sea.

If the child continues to be very restless have him lie down on his back, legs and arms straight during the meditation. There is a danger he may fall asleep. It's better for him to learn how to meditate sitting up and to practice the yoga relaxation exercises before meditating until he can be still while sitting up. Another possibility for very restless children is to have them move their bodies and sway like the sea and the waves and gradually calm down to perfect still-ness. Continue to slowly increase the time the child sits immersed in the stillness before going on.

The circle and dot meditation on p. 111 is a good one for children this age and can be done along with the sea relaxa-tion or at another time. After the meditation, discuss what the colors meant to the child. Is there something in the room that's the same color as what you saw? Can you draw what you saw? Look around at the other people. Do any of them have any of those colors you saw around them?

MEDITATION WITH SIX TO TEN YEAR OLDS

This age group is ready to learn more self-discipline. Most of these children will be in first through fifth grade. They are looking for challenges and enjoy doing a variety of things. Concentration exercises should be repeated daily to teach the child how to delve deeply into whatever he may be doing. They can be varied to keep the exercises fun. In Chapter 6 there are a variety of concentration exercises to practice. One type of concentration exercise good for this age is to use a watch with a second hand and concentrate on the second hand as it goes around the dial. Do not let any-thing distract, any noises or any thoughts or fidgeting. Try not to blink. See how long you can do it, being perfectly still. A child can be taught how to tell time while doing this exercise. Make a chart with the date and how long the period of concentration was so you can watch improve-ment. Try to lengthen the concentration each day, but don't be surprised if some days are more difficult than others, or if it appears to be going backward and getting worse for a few days. Look for an overall increase. This same exercise can be done by looking at a candle flame or even a cloud. Cloud gazing can turn into a meditation as the mind begins to drift with the cloud as it forms shapes and figures. See how many different shapes you can see in the cloud.

Six to ten year olds haven't really developed the mind

yet. They relate through their own feelings, through unconsciously absorbing feelings from others, through imitating adults and each other, through picking up unconscious impressions, and through developing their five senses. They will especially enjoy the exercises that involve their senses.

It is important not to instill competition between the children as they do these exercises. Instead we must emphasize that they are competing only with their own self. Sometimes one child will feel upset because Johnny can do it and he can't. He may even refuse to participate. It is helpful to make a chart of his own improvements. This record gives him an incentive to put in the effort needed to improve and to feel good about himself. Simple rewards for improving himself may help him have more desire to continue improving.

Children in this age group also need to follow up meditation with activity to ground their energies. Art or craft projects requiring concentration and projects done with one or both parents are ways of creatively using the energy that can help bring the depth of the meditations into the outer expression. The child himself will often be surprised how much more creative he can be when meditation is done regularly. We found this increase in creativity and self-image starting to occur almost immediately in one public school classroom where meditation was introduced to a group of ten year olds for only a two-week period. The child may also be surprised at how much brighter the world looks or how much closer he feels to family and friends after the meditation.

Often there is a big difference between the inner life and the outer expression in children. There may be emotions churning inside and a quiet, unexpressive personality outside, repressing the inner feelings. Or there may be a highly emotional and disruptive personality outside as well as inside which is coming out and showing some inner insecurity. We have to learn to see how the outer manifestation is related to what's going on inside in order to guide our children.

Children six to ten should be able to meditate at least five to ten minutes once they learn the technique of how to go deep enough so that it feels good. Then the meditation will hold them there. But, in the beginning it will take self-discipline to control the body and the moods. Occasionally a child may really get into the depths of himself and sit for twenty or thirty minutes. A lot of awakening can be happening inside in that silence.

Whereas adults can sit for twenty to thirty minutes and not get beyond their own mind-tapes spinning around with memories and thoughts, children sitting that long will probably be in a much deeper, mindless realm. They don't have the accumulated memories, associations and patterns in the mind that bog down most adults.

Children need also to be encouraged to explore the depths in nature, to get inside the rock or the bird or the wind. Short, but deep meditations alternating with activity are more suited to most children's temperaments and are far better than longer restless meditations.

Science now intellectually recognizes that all is energy and all matter is energy crystallized into mass and form. But few scientists have directly experienced this reality in their beings. That our consciousness and energy and light are all the same is something science has not yet discovered with its instruments, but it is what is seen and understood through meditation and awareness expansion. Children experience energies flowing in and through and around them while meditating. They can quickly learn to see energy flowing as light in all forms and experience different qualities of energy in whatever they do. Many of the awareness exercises are for the purpose of becoming aware of how energies move inside us, and between us and other people, in nature and between physical objects. That all is energy and (all interactions between anything is energy) is the main unfolding awareness that a child begins to experience directly when he meditates. Then gradually he can begin to connect the energy in himself with whatever activity he is doing.

Learning how to really listen is also part of concentration. How to listen to others, listen to nature, listen to ourself and what is going on inside of us is a must if we are going to be true to ourself. This is the pristine inner silence, the primal innocence that young children are usually in touch with before feelings become repressed. It is the primal innocence of the Adam and Eve state of consciousness in the Garden of Eden, before the fall into confusion and disorder. It means being in touch with our True Self.

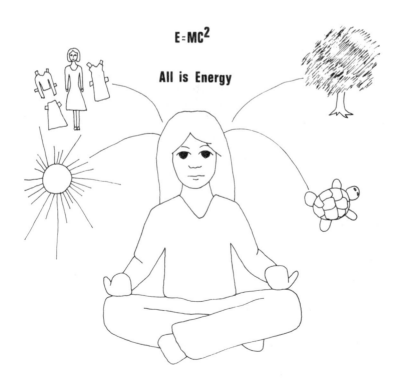

A MEDITATION EXERCISE FOR SIX TO TEN YEAR OLDS

Begin the same as for three to five year olds with the sea relaxation.

Now that we are quiet and relaxed and perfectly still, let us imagine that we're at the top of a tall building and we're going to walk down the staircase to the ground floor. We are putting one foot down after the other and it is a long staircase. We are going down, down, down, one step at a time. 1 . . . 2 . . . 3 . . . 4 . . . 5 . . . 6 . . . 7 . . . 8 . . . 9 . . . 10 . . . Now we turn the corner and go down another stairway. 1 . . . 2 . . . 3 . . . 4 . . . 5 . . . 6 . . . 7 . . . 8 . . . 9 . . . 10 . . . And now we keep going, one step after the other . . . 1 . . . 2 . . . 3 . . . 4 . . . 5 . . . 6 . . . 7 . . . 8 . . . 9 . . . 10 . . . And now we are at the bottom and there is a trap door leading into our heart. We open the door and walk inside our own heart. *Listen* . . . to what your heart is telling you . . . Ask it a question, to yourself, not out-loud . . . *Listen* for the answer. Be sure to ask your question.

(*Pause* before going on.) Now, very quiet. Feel your toes. Imagine that your toes are disappearing, vanishing into the air. Now, feel your feet. Feel them disappear into the light around . . . No feet, only light . . . Feel your ankles and feel them vanish, disappear. Now your legs are vanishing. Feel your knees and feel them disappear, dissolve into atoms and energy. Imagine your buttocks and stomach disappear, dissolving into light. Imagine your buttocks and stomach disappear into light, dissolved in the air. Feel your chest and feel it totally disappear. And now the arms . . . they're so light they are disappearing. Feel your shoulders and feel them vanish into light. Feel your chin and feel it dissolve— And now imagine your mouth and cheeks and nose dissolve into pure energy, into light. Your eyes and forehead are disappearing and now the very top of your head has dissapeared into light . . . there is no body left, it has entirely disappeared.

All of its atoms have dissolved into pure energy— light— nothing. There is nothing left, just your real Self. Nothing left but your awareness— that came to earth when you were born to live, work, play and grow in your body. But you had forgotten who you really are. You began to believe you were your body. Now do you remember what it's like to have no body? Who are you? Are you space? (This exercise can also be done lying down, before bedtime or, if the child is restless, during the meditation.)

Let's slowly remake our bodies now and imagine all our flesh and bones and blood and organs come back to us. Let's imagine our senses returning— our touch— we can feel our bones and muscles again. Our taste— we can sense the taste of our own mouth again— our smell— we can smell our body and we can smell the room— our hearing— we can hear more and more sounds. We can hear our breathing, the voices are louder. What else can we hear? Now last of all our sight. Let's open our eyes and look around. What's the first thing you see? Do things look different?

AWARENESS EXERCISE

One person will have to prepare the materials beforehand and guide the session. It's fun to do the exercise blindfolded, then we haven't any temptation to open our eyes early and we get deeper into the experience. Blindfolds can easily be made from an old torn up sheet.

Concentrate on touching, one at a time, five different objects. (For example, a cotton ball, a rough rock, a dandelion, a pillow, water.) How do they feel? Really feel them. Can you tell what they are?

Listen carefully. Name ten different sounds you can hear.

List as many different smells in the house as you are old

up to fifteen. (The guide can lead the blindfolded person around the house. Put him near an open window to smell the outdoors too.)

Taste five different things. Really taste them. (Like sugar, salt, cream, soda, bread.) Can you guess what they are?

Blindfolds off. Go into each room in the house. Decide what color is most common in each room. Then go into one room only and try to remember everything in it. Go out of the room and list everything you remember seeing in it from memory. (Children who can't write can say what they remember outloud to the guide.) Now draw the room and place everything on your list in it. Try to list and draw at least as many things as you are old.

This exercise can also be done outdoors. If there are many children who can't write, modify the exercise to suit their needs, or have several guides. Older children can rotate as guides. It must be made clear to the guides that this is also a trust exercise and they are responsible for seeing that their blindfolded person doesn't trip over or crash into things. It's very important that we not play tricks, but work to deepen the trust.

MEDITATION WITH ELEVEN
TO FIFTEEN YEAR OLDS

Children eleven to fifteen years old are going through puberty. Any meditation given for them must keep this change in mind. The minds of children this age are beginning to really develop as is the ability to truly reason and discriminate. These changes are often accompanied by dramatic personality changes and some of the patterns fixed in puberty remain for the rest of life. It is often an emotionally traumatic time. Most of the emotions are kept inside, appearing outwardly as increased moodiness, maybe rebelliousness or explosiveness. If a child this age can learn to be open, is able to trust and to share, he will have fewer problems. Social pressures from peers begin to be a greater influence during this time, usually because feelings are not shared in the home, and there is not a strong Centered feeling. Many eleven to fifteen year olds are already smoking cigarettes, and experimenting with drugs and sex.

Meditation for this age group is essential to create a center of peace amidst all the changes. At this age the mind can begin to see causes and effects of actions clearly. Awareness sessions for this age group need to look into these causes and effects. They need to be more psychological. They especially need to show how to feel what another is feeling, how to be able to look from the other's point of view, and how to express real feelings. Usually from age eleven through adulthood self-obsession with personal problems increases which blocks sensitivity to others. Awareness exercises that help clear miscommunications are very important for teenagers. Once the mind begins to take hold and the sexual energies begin to color feelings, our view of life becomes more filtered.

Unless the mind is trained to look into why we are like we are and unless sex feelings are handled rather than repressed, our perspective on life is going to be twisted in some way. So we need to learn how to open and keep the channels of communication clear by discussing feelings and problems with each other and by looking into our inner motives and desires. An understanding of the male-female psychic energies in our body is also important. We are all both male and female in that we have both energies operating in us. By learning how to handle these energies and use them we gain control of our sexuality rather than be tossed around by it.

Values clarification classes are being taught to children this age in some public schools. But how rare it is for children to be able to sort out their values in the home, or even be really open about what they feel about sex in school or at home. Most adults are confused about sex themselves and unable to really give helpful advice in that area. It is real feelings that children, this age especially, are interested in getting into, and few adults or children feel their real feelings are acceptable. The first step we have to take is to accept ourself and our feelings, sexual and otherwise, as natural and okay. Then we can begin to feel all right about discussing them with others who accept their own feelings as well as ours as real.

Puberty opens new psychic energies, emotional changes and, as a result, different ways of looking at life. These have to be understood by the child for his own good. Psychic phenomena are said to occur frequently around children of this age because of these new energies.

It is in this age group and through age eighteen that major conflicts with parents emerge openly. Parents' problems often conflict with teenagers' problems even though they may really be based on the same need. A mother who fears rejection may want her daughter to be popular and moralistic, which is Mother's idea of what is accepted. The daughter, who fears rejection too, may decide to go along with the crowd that smokes, drinks and takes drugs in order to feel accepted. If Mother finds out she becomes angered and feels her daughter has rejected her, and that society will reject them both. Daughter is angered, too, feeling that she can't tell Mother anything. She has to hide from her because Mother won't accept her. Result: Poor communication. This pattern, in different degrees, is more common than not between parents and children during the teenage years.

We absorb many of our parents psychological tendencies as we identify with them in our early years. Often we end up repeating old patterns and building up more problems, more karma, during our lives.

As discussed in Chapter 1, working through this karma, these challenges for our growth will eventually help us gain true wisdom. Frequently parents and children have similar tendencies which they see and dislike in each other. We don't realize it is our own problem we are reacting to. The teenage years in particular offer a fertile environment for confronting and working through these problems. It is through mastering these challenges and gaining the wisdom that the soul's lessons are learned and love becomes pure. Once we have reached the inner Source we will see through our patterns and filters and be able to deal effectively with them. Learning this while still in our childhood or teenage years enables us to be master of ourself throughout life. We can then use our knowledge to help the rest of humanity become liberated.

In order to achieve this we need to learn how to see through our patterns to be rid of them. Evolution is very slow and identification with psychological patterns is very strong. Through meditation, doing the wisdom, we speed up the process of evolution and transfer identification to the higher Self, away from our karmic patterns. The light of the True Self illumines and helps us see through the patterns, at the same time pulling us rapidly along the evolutionary energy stream.

Even the touchiest teenage problems can be considered from the cause and effect angle of karma. In this new light we shift from the right-wrong judgmental attitude which causes rebellion, to an attitude of looking at our responsibilities. Even after foreseeing the possible consequences of his actions, a child may still decide to take his own risks and learn through mistakes, but at least he has been made aware of his responsibility. If as parents we say, "I feel you are smoking just to look good with your friends, to be in with the crowd. Smoking can really ruin your health. So it is more important to you to be accepted by your friends than it is to take care of your body. How do you feel about it?" Then we are seeing things as they are. After all feelings are openly shared, then any disciplinary action on the parent's part will be perfectly clear to the child. Life will eventually show him if the parents can't. Parents can help guide children by setting an example, sharing their wisdom and feelings, and pointing out the causes and effects of attitudes and actions. They can discipline, but in the end they must leave the children with freedom to choose. Love, trust and respect are preserved in this way and the parental guidance is in harmony with nature's own method.

Children of this age group can meditate for long periods since their concentration ability is developed more than younger children. However, if they are having problems they may find it more difficult to quiet the mind and emotions than younger children. They will need to do some physical yoga exercises to quiet and balance their rapidly growing and restless energies in order to be comfortable while sitting still. By this age they are often less limber than the younger children and the puberty energies are likely to make them even more physically restless. They need to become more aware of what's happening to their internal energies. The spine stretching exercises are very good for releasing energy blocks.

With the increase in drug usage by children of this age and older, something should be said about the effects of some drugs on the consciousness. Psychedelic drugs have been popular because they act on the nervous system to present an altered view of life. Psychedelic means mind expanding and they do remove inhibiting blocks to release the creative imagination. Whether the use is constructive or destructive depends on the individual. The *urge* to use the creative imagination and expand the mind is natural and evolutionary. Our modern culture has restricted and hemmed in this natural faculty and drug taking is a reaction to it. Drug taking is a compensation for some lack or unfulfillment. In the exercises given here, a safe, natural way to develop the imagination and expand the mind is presented, without the unnatural and often harmful forcing effects that drugs produce.

A MEDITATION EXERCISE FOR
ELEVEN TO FIFTEEN YEAR OLDS

Do several of the yoga postures to tone and relax the physical body. Be sure to include a spine stretching exercise among them. Try to really feel the energies release and flow through the body as you exercise. Note which side was easier to stretch, the right or the left? For most males the right side is easier and for most females the left side is easier, especially after puberty. This is because we have both male and female energies in us. The left side of the body and spine channels the female, receptive energy, while the right side of the body and spine channels the male, aggressive, dynamic energies. Learning how to balance the male-female energies inside us can help us handle our sexual energies that are strong in puberty and are with us throughout life.

The breath flows through one nostril more strongly than the other at any time during the day, except when the breath is switching from one nostril to the other, then there is equal flow. This switch takes place about every fifty-five minutes except when there is an imbalance, then it remains longer on the side that is stronger. When the breath is flowing more through the right nostril, then the masculine dynamic energy is strong in the personality. When it flows more through the left nostril, then the female passive energy is stronger. For sexual balance, the goal is to balance the flows.

If there are pronounced female tendencies or appearances in a male, then there is a need to strengthen the right side; and conversely, if there are pronounced male tendencies or appearances in a female, there is a need to strengthen the left side. If a person is troubled by being oversexed, this can be helped by strengthening the opposite side, the passive left side if male and the aggressive right side if female. Balancing can be done by blocking one nostril to increase the energy flow in the other nostril. Do not force blocking for long periods if it is uncomfortable. Build it up gradually, remembering that balance is the desired aim.

Regardless of what sex you are, you can learn to use and master these energies. It takes practice to know how to put enough consciousness into the exercises to have them work at our command to balance out these powerful energies.

The sex act itself balances the energies in the body. So does proper meditation. When the flow is equal between both nostrils, which happens at the high, still point during meditation, then the energy is most powerful and whatever thought we think then will have more power behind it to manifest. This is why it is important to have only pure thoughts in meditation. The same is true for the sex act where the energies balance and discharge. It is important to hold only pure thoughts during the sexual act because those energies are extremely powerful and whatever is in the mind and being will be manifested by the powerful kundalini energy release. Remember, energy follows thought. Many couples who have problems with each other or hold resentments carry these feelings and thoughts into the sex act where they are reinforced by the powerful energies, unconsciously making matters even worse! The thoughts that follow the sex act are a good reflection of where we are really at, what is really going on inside us. When male and female come together in sex they ideally balance each other's energies which gives the good feeling and the sense of well-being. If one or both partners is left unsatisfied, there is some block in the energy so it doesn't get balanced. Usually the block is emotional or psychological. The following breathing exercise also serves to balance the energies and should be practiced regularly until you have learned to identify the two different energy flows.

Sit up with spine straight in a comfortable position. With the little finger of the right hand, block off the left nostril by pressing gently against the cartilage. Inhale, to a count of six, through the right nostril. Block off the right nostril by pressing the thumb gently against the cartilage, hold the breath to a count of six. Lift off the little finger but keep the right nostril blocked. Exhale to a count of six through the left nostril. Then inhale through the left nostril to a count of six. Block the left nostril again with the little finger and hold to a count of six. Unblock the right nostril and exhale to a count of six. Inhale through the right nostril to a count of six. Repeat ten times and imagine and feel the energies balancing in the body. Feel them moving in your spine. Imagine them moving like a current along either side of the spine until you can feel it. Sit calmly when you've finished the exercise, enjoying the balanced feeling. Practice this until you can feel the different quality of the two energies. Then, when you want to be more receptive you can bring in more female energy at will by blocking the right nostril. When you want to get something done and be more dynamic, you can bring in more male energy by blocking the left nostril.

Another guide is to look in the mirror, or look into another's eyes. Which eye is larger or stronger? It may change from time to time. The stronger eye is on the side of the dominant energy in that person, at that time.

After relaxing the body and balancing the male-female energies through the previous exercise, sit up straight in meditation posture and prepare for the following meditation to go into the Center within. Breathe rhythmically and concentrate on the spiritual eye at the point between the eyebrows behind the forehead, deep inside.

SPACESHIP MEDITATION

Imagine there is a spaceship inside of your head. Step inside your spaceship right in the center of your head. Note what color it is. Feel it take off and go all the way through the top of your head, up, up, up, past millions of planets and stars on its way up, up, up . . . (pause) . . . keep going up, forever . . . observe what you see . . . now go all the way up in your spaceship . . . down, down, down, down . . . down, through the center of the earth and out the other side, down, down, down, . . . forever . . . down . . . now, go up again, up, up, up, all the way up, higher and farther this time, up, up, up, now go all the way to the left . . . farther and farther . . . forever to the left . . . now all the way to the right . . . farther, farther, farther, farther . . . what do you see?

Now come back to center space station and go all the way forward, straight in front, straight on, farther, farther, farther, farther . . . what do you hear? . . . farther, and now go all the way back, behind, back, back, farther back, on and on, farther and farther, deeper back . . . Now come back slowly to the center . . . and come back in to the top of your head and now you are inside your head again. Step out of your spaceship. You have traveled over and through the entire universe. Open your eyes; look around you. What did you see in your universe? Meditate on the whole universe as something you experience inside your own awareness, inside your own consciousness . . .

For everyone over fifteen years, all the meditations in the book can be used. These age groupings are not for the purpose of setting limits, rather they are to serve as general guidelines on how to bring meditation to children of different ages, with differing needs. Everyone of any age can enjoy the meditations and exercises for the younger children. It's a good idea to begin with them and work up to the more complicated ones. Really it doesn't matter how simple an exercise is, it is the experience of expanded awareness and sensitivity that we want. The exercises for preschoolers may even be more rewarding for some because of their simplicity. Practice them all with your children, your friends and alone. Similarly, a five year old may enjoy exercises listed for ten year olds. Let the child describe his or her own limits by including him as much as possible to see what he accepts and what he rejects, rather than imposing our ideas of what his limits are on him.

Children over fifteen years are beginning to look more deeply into their personal life goals and into fulfilling personal desires. Introducing awareness expansion at this time in life can give a greater capacity to fulfill their aims as well as build healthy attitudes that will shape the direction of life.

For all age groups concentration, flowering the creative imagination and developing fine sensory and extrasensory perception are emphasized. An added emphasis for older children is probing into the causes behind their own feelings and others' feelings, behind their own actions and others' actions. As we continue to grow we begin to see deeply into nature's cycles, the causes behind social pressures and the need for attention to maintaining balance in nature (ecology) and in ourselves. After all, we are part of nature too. The deeper the ability to concentrate one-pointedly, the deeper will be the true intuitive understanding of life. The inner life makes the outer life and it is within that we need to re-educate our children and ourselves.

DIFFERING FAMILY NEEDS

Let's put ourself into different family models to discover more about how to meditate as a group.

Model A.   In the first family model there is a mother and father who have never meditated before. There are two children, ages six and eight. The way to begin is for the mother and father to start meditating alone and together to get the feel of what it means. They also practice a few of the exercises together. When they feel they have a good grasp of how to do it and are able to achieve a centered feeling within themselves, then it is time to include the children. This preparation may take a week or a month, but it is necessary as it will provide a foundation for the children. When the parents are ready, they choose a time for a daily family meditation, say, for example, in the early evening. Two or three times a week, as often as it fits their schedule, they also add one of the awareness exercises to the meditation. Some of these exercises need prior preparation. They try to make time to really share feelings and discover what has been going on inside each other during these sessions. They choose exercises from the book that can include the six and eight year old. After the children are in bed, they go on to an exercise between just the two of them.

Model B.   In the second family, there is a mother and

father who have meditated, and they have four children, ages four, ten, twelve, fifteen. Here the mother and father already have some idea of what centering means. After some practice at becoming familiar with the meditations and exercises given here, they begin to include the children. Again, they choose a time for the daily family meditation and plan the family awareness sessions ahead of time. They begin with an exercise that can include the four year old. Then they go on to a more involved awareness activity with the three older children after the four year old is in bed or busy elsewhere. During the day sometime, the mother or father meditates and does some of the exercises with the four year old tailored to her needs and attention span.

Model C.   Our third family has a mother and father who have been religious and church-going, though they have never practiced true meditation. They have a large family, ages two, five, seven, eight, eleven and sixteen. Here the parents should find a time to begin meditations and awareness exercises. Then, when they feel ready, they introduce them to the children. Here we have a very wide age range with very different needs. A family group meditation will not be able to include the two year old for more than a few minutes. Even the five year old may want to wriggle alot. The best approach is to have a family meditation for just a few minutes, gently encouraging the two year old ahead of time to be still, and then to find somewhere else for the two year old and probably the five year old to be. One parent may have to take them while the other parent continues with the other four. At different times during the week the parents can meditate and practice awareness exercises with the children individually or in pairs based on age. For example, the parents and the eleven and sixteen year old may work together at one time. At another time just the parents and the sixteen year old. Another time the seven, nine and eleven year old and the parents. With practice they will discover their own best combinations and times.

Model D.   The fourth family example is a single parent

with any number of children. The single parent usually finds the task of childraising very difficult. Usually the parent is restless, wanting a mate or busy with work and activities away from home. Meditating together at a set time daily may seem impossible, but, with enough planning and firmness it can be done. The single parent must learn how to center, before bringing the children into the meditation, or all that he or she will be conveying to the children will be the parent's own scatteredness or restlessness. Having a strong Center is the most important thing a single parent can give to the children, as they have only her or him to identify with.

Whenever possible, single parents and their families should get together to share their problems and their growth and to do the awareness exercises. They can help reinforce each other, and the presence of another strong, centered adult is very beneficial for the children's need for security.

Families with both parents can also find that added strength and fresh insight comes from getting together with another family for mutual sharing. It helps everyone to see outside the family blindnesses.

Chapter 5

Yoga Exercises for the Young

The real purpose of yoga exercises is to put the body in a state where meditation on the One is possible. If the body is restless or aching, our attention will keep wandering to its pulls instead of meditating. Yoga exercises also help us to become more sensitive to how energy flows and gets blocked in the body.

If we have physical tensions and pains then there are blocks in the nerves or muscles and energy will not flow freely. Physical tensions are usually related to mental and emotional tensions, which yoga exercises help us get in touch with; then we can release them. As we practice, we experience mind and body as one, not separate. The body eventually manifests whatever is happening in the mind and emotions, whether joy and health or hurts and pains.

Physical yoga is called hatha yoga. Hatha means sun-moon, and hatha yoga is balancing the spiritual and physical and male and female energies (the polarities) in the body. These exercises are excellent for people of any age to keep their health in a general state of ease. They were developed thousands of years ago in ancient India for the purpose of tuning the body to nature's balance, and to help the meditation process. Just as a guitar must be tuned to pitch in order to produce a harmonious, resonant sound, so must the body be tuned to nature to do the same. Those who practice hatha yoga regularly generally experience fewer illnesses. The internal body energies are continuously toned and become resistant to infection. When the body is in a state of ease, it is difficult for disease to enter.

The recharging exercises, given first, develop the will and concentration in directing energy in and through the body. By practicing these exercises we learn how to recharge the body with fresh life force drawn from prana, or vital currents, which circulate in the air around us. Any time we are in need of more energy we can tap the life force and give ourself a charge, just as if we are recharging an automobile battery with electric current. The body is a wet cell battery that takes in and stores vital energy. It is wise to practice some of these exercises daily, preferably preceding your meditation time. Exercise until you feel relaxed enough so you can sit still in meditation without the mind going to the tugging legs or aching back. If you want to go more deeply into hatha yoga, beyond the simple exercises presented here, there are many instructional books available. The principles behind the recharging exercises were drawn from Paramahansa Yogananda's exercises developed in 1917.

YOGA RECHARGING EXERCISES

Step 1.   Stand up straight, feet together, hands relaxed at the sides. Close the eyes and concentrate at the center between the brows inside the head. Try to get balanced there between your left side and right side, as if you are balancing on ice skates. Continue to focus your attention at that point and imagine you are drawing in currents of energy through the top of your head and through the back of your neck. Use your will and your imagination to direct the energy to flow down your whole body into your left foot as you tense the left foot and then relax it. As you repeat, you will feel

the energy moving into your brain, down your body to the foot. Imagine and tense. Let the foot vibrate gently for a few seconds and relax it. Imagine the energy has dissolved any tensions and brought in fresh life force to the foot. Feel your foot tingling a bit.

Do the same with your right foot. Proceed in the same manner all the way up the body in this order: left foot, right foot, left calf, right calf, left knee, right knee, left thigh, right thigh, left buttock, right buttock, abdomen, stomach, left chest, right chest, left shoulder, right shoulder, left upper arm, right upper arm, left lower arm, right lower arm, left hand, right hand, left half of neck, right half of neck, face, scalp, then the entire body at once. Imagine the life energy flowing in, will it to flow in, tense the whole body gently until it vibrates like a motor, then slowly relax. This exercise will recharge the entire body to the degree that you are able to stay concentrated, and use your will and imagination vividly to direct this energy. You can even do this exercise mentally with good results if you are unable to actually tense the body part due to pain or paralysis. When any body part is diseased or weak, or in pain, you can very gently send life-force to it in this way to help it heal.

Be sure to concentrate on directly feeling the fresh energy as it flows to the different body parts. It may feel like electrical tingles. As you practice you will develop concentration, will, imagination and awareness of energy as well as break up energy blocks, relax and tone muscles and nerves. Recharging can also be extended to the following variations. These are not calisthenics. The use of the will, sensitivity and imagination are even more important for an integration of body and mind than is the physical tensing and relaxing. Remember to do all parts of the exercises. By removing energy blocks, these exercises provide for a more relaxed sleep at night as well. Use the same basic method given in Step 1 with the other variations. Pause between each exercise to feel what the energy has done to you.

Step 2.   Roll the head loosely on the neck five times one

way, stretching it all the way around, but never straining. Repeat going five times the other way.

Step 3.   Hold the arms straight out horizontally from the body. Twist them like an airplane to the left while you twist the hips to the right. Then swing the hips to the left and the arms to the right. Feel your spine twisting. Do this ten times on each side, lowering your arms to waist level and back up to shoulder level as you proceed, making sure that the entire spine is stretched.

Step 4.   Put your hands on your waist, feet slightly apart. Keeping the spine straight, roll the torso around the waist, leaning forward, then to the right, then to the back, then to the left, and back to the front. Repeat five times in each direction.

Step 5.   Gently rap your entire head with your fists. Eyes closed, will your brain cells to wake up. Wake up brain cells! Imagine energy flowing into the brain and gently stimulating the brain cells and nerves to greater activity. Then massage your entire head and scalp gently with your fingertips. Feel as though you are massaging life energy into the brain.

Step 6.   Walk in place lifting the left knee high with the right arm bent. Then lift the right knee high toward the chest and bend the left arm. Step in place fifteen times.

Step 7.   Run in place. Touch the heels to the buttocks. Run in place fifteen times.

Remember, the more you can stay concentrated the better the results.

YOGA POSTURES

In all these postures there are several points to remember.

When it says jump two or three feet apart, these distances will have to be reduced for little bodies.

Stretch, but never strain. Go only as far as you can. Each day will show some improvement if you practice regularly.

On inhalations draw in energy. On exhalations let energy out and stretch a little further. *Stretch only on exhalations.* Go slow and be patient with yourself. It's better to go slow and do the exercise properly. Your patience will bring self-mastery.

Relax in The Corpse Posture for awhile when you are finished. Don't jump up right away. Feel the new balance within you and take it with you into your meditation or your next activity.

The Tree   Stand upright, feet together, Pretend you are a marionette— a puppet with a string holding your head and back up straight. Find a point on the wall directly in front of you. Concentrate on that point and don't take your eyes off of it. It will help you keep your balance. As you concentrate, raise your right foot and place it on your left knee. Bend the right knee out toward the right. Raise your arms up over your head. Straighten the arms, palms touching. Bring the arms in line with your ears. Inhale, exhale and push your pelvis down as you stretch your arms up higher. Inhale again and as you exhale let the shoulders down, at the same time stretch the arms still higher. Stay in this position a minute. Inhale and come down on the exhalation. Repeat on the other side. With practice you will be able to do this posture well.

Spinal Twist   Lie flat on the back, arms horizontally straight out, legs together. Turn the head to the left. Put the left foot on top of the right knee, put the right hand on top of the left knee. Keeping the head turned left and the left shoulder on the ground, bring the left knee close to the ground on the right side of the right leg. Don't strain, just inhale, then on the exhalation relax and stretch. Stretch only on the exhalations. Again, inhale, relax, exhale, relax and stretch and feel the body give more into the posture.

Imagine yourself totally relaxed in the full posture even if you can't quite do it yet— with both the left knee and left shoulder on the ground. Your visualizing and imagining will help you get there. Again, inhale, relax, exhale and relax and stretch. Your bones may make a noise as your muscles stretch.

Now inhale and come to center lying on your back. Feel the difference between the left and right sides of your body. Feel how the energy flows more freely on the stretched side. Now do the same thing on the other side. Turn the head to the right. Put the right foot on top of the left knee, put the left hand on top of the right knee. Keeping the head turned right and the right shoulder on the ground, bring the right knee close to the ground on the left side of the left leg. Again, stretch on the exhalation only. Don't strain, just exhale, relax and stretch. When you're through, feel your whole body relaxed. Which side was it easier to stretch, the right or left? For males the right side is usually easier, for females the left side.

The Cobra Snake   Lie face down on the floor with the hands palms down by the shoulders, elbows on the ground. Inhale and raise up the chest, exhale and straighten the arms and bend back, keeping the head up and shoulders down. Put your awareness in your spine and on each exhalation bend a bit more from the base of the spine up to the neck. Keep the stomach down and the legs on the floor. Exhale and come down slowly. Relax.

The Shoulder Stand   Lie flat on the floor on your back, heels forward, palms down. Inhale, then exhale and raise the legs slowly until they are straight up in the air. Place the hands, palms flat, on the back to support the legs. Keep the elbows in. Walk the hands up the spine until the back is straight up and the legs are straight up. Tuck the chin in and look at the chest. Keep the waist in and keep stretching up, with the soles of the feet parallel to the ceiling. Hold for a few minutes. Don't strain. Come down slowly. Relax.

(Women should avoid this posture, or any other upside down postures during menstrual periods.)

The Woodchopper   Stand upright with feet two feet apart, arms over the head, hands clasped. Inhale and move arms backward over the head. Bend back as if you are swinging an axe back. Exhale as you bring arms forward and down quickly, yelling HA! just as though you were chopping a log with an axe. Repeat three or four times. This is a good exercise for cleansing the lungs.

The Triangle   Stand up straight, feet together, arms at the side. Balance the body between the left and right sides. Inhale and as you exhale jump so the feet are three feet apart, arms and hands out to the sides, level with the shoulders. Turn the left foot inward and the right foot outward. Inhale and as you exhale bend sideways to touch the right ankle with the right hand. Look up at the left hand which is pointing upward, palm facing the front. Take one or two breaths and open up the chest. Inhale and come up. Repeat on the other side turning the right foot inward and the left foot outward. When you are through, inhale and as you exhale jump bringing the feet together and arms back down.

The Dog   Lie on the floor, stomach down, hands by the waist, palms pressing against the floor. Spread feet about one foot apart, heels in the air and toes on the ground. Inhale and raise the chest, pushing up on the hands. Without moving hands or toes, exhale and push back onto the heels, straightening the legs and arms and lifting hips high bringing the chest toward the knees. Relax head and neck. Breathe normally. On each exhalation use your will and move into a more perfect posture. Lie back down.

Head to Toe   Sit upright with legs outstretched, heels forward. Keep the back of the knees on the floor and keep the spine straight with head up. Reach forward as far as you can without straining. Hold on to the toes or as far down the

legs as you can reach. (You can use a towel around the feet and pull on the ends of it if you like.) Inhale and observe the body, exhale and stretch up the spine, drawing in the waist and taking the shoulders back. Take one or two breaths in this position. Inhale, observe the body again, and as you exhale, slowly bring the chest toward the knees, but keep a straight spine. Remember to stretch only on the exhalations. Go as far as you can without straining, keeping the head up as you bring the chest to the knees. Inhale and come up.

The Lion   Kneel with hands on the knees, spine straight. Put the tongue on the upper palate. Inhale deeply. Lean over and roll the tongue out of the mouth stretching it forward. Force every bit of air from the lungs with a ferocious lion's roar. Look ferocious as you roar. Inhale and sit up and repeat. This exercise helps to clear the lungs.

Eek and Ook   Kneel with hands on the knees, spine straight. Form the word *eek* with your mouth and stretch your whole face, eyes, cheeks and mouth into a big *eeeeeek*. This stretches the whole face sideways. Then form the mouth into the sound *ook,* stretching the lips forward and drawing the whole face, eyebrows and neck forward, into a mad *oooooook*. Repeat several times. A good exercise for loosening up the entire face.

The Corpse   Lie flat on the back, feet relaxed, hands facing upward. Make sure the shoulders, buttocks and legs are evenly resting upon the floor. Close the eyes. Feel your body revitalized and fresh after all the other postures. Feel the mind in harmony with the body and enjoy the peace. Be so relaxed that you really feel you are lying like a corpse. For further relaxation, imagine your muscles and flesh falling off your bones, so there's only a skeleton left . . . Imagine the bones disintegrating into atoms and flying away into space . . . Nothing is left . . . but your awareness.

Chapter 6

Concentration and Meditation

The importance of relaxation and of developing good concentration for self-mastery cannot be overstated. True meditation can begin only when we are able to concentrate our consciousness and there are no distractions. Being able to concentrate the mind allows us to direct energy where we want it and when we want it. Whether we are trying to follow a deep train of thought, trying not to spill a cup brimming with hot tea, or trying to still our thoughts, we need to be able to concentrate to succeed.

Concentration is not achieved by straining or forcing the mind. It can only be accomplished when the mind is relaxed and poised. It comes with using the will to focus our attention and interest so it is absorbed in only one thing at a time. A balance is needed between directed will and relaxation to achieve sustained concentration. We can practice the following concentration exercises to develop the skill. Then we need to learn to apply the skill throughout the day, so our entire attitude reflects it. Deep concentration is like focusing consciousness into a laser beam that is so high-energy and intense it can see right through to the real meanings behind people's behavior, behind people's thoughts and behind life.

When practicing the concentration exercises we must patiently and continually bring our mind back to our point of concentration every time it starts to wander. With persistence we will gradually increase our ability to concentrate. We will begin to watch ourselves and our children perceiving more clearly and more deeply.

Concentration is the first step and meditation the second step. Meditation expands the consciousness from the central point of concentration to include and become aware of the whole. The third step, after meditation, is dissolving our sense of being a separate I, an ego or personality, and merging into the whole until we are one with it. Then there is no separation, no difference. It's very difficult to maintain this third step for very long. Our ego will return to trip us up until we have worked through our ego blocks— our projections, assumptions, filters and mind patterns. These can be seen in our day-to-day living. There are many levels of merging into the One. Only when the ego is completely dissolved are we in a state of Pure Consciousness.

The creative imagination can take us anywhere. All it takes is exercising it. Lying in bed at night we can imagine ourself sitting on top of the house roof looking through the treetops at the stars above. We can even imagine a delicate breeze caressing our body, brushing across our cheeks. It feels soft, sweet and real. We use the imagination unconsciously all the time for wishing, hoping and fearing. Often we make our images come true by putting so much energy into them. We need to make our images constructive and creative and put enough consciousness behind them to re-create our reality into something better for ourselves. When the image-making faculty and the will work together they are so powerful they can actually create what we imagine. That is why we must be careful about what we want and we need to root out fears and doubts or else they will come true too. Just like learning arithmetic in school, we have to practice. We practice creatively imagining and putting energy constructively into helpful directions over and over to make the images real in our lives. The meditations following the concentration exercises help develop the creative imagination needed to expand consciousness and gain more control over our lives.

When preparing for a complete session by yourself or with your family, plan to begin with some of the physical exercises, then a concentration exercise, then proceed to a meditation, and then to an awareness activity. If time is limited you won't be able to include all of these, of course. Choose what you feel is needed most in your situation.

CONCENTRATION EXERCISES

1.   Light a candle and place it in the center of a table or the center of the floor. Sit around it in a circle, not too close. Concentrate on the candle flame. Imagine you are sitting in the center of the flame. Feel yourself melting into the flame. Let it consume you. Feel its nature. Imagine everyone else in the circle is sitting inside the flame too, melted into the flame. We are all one flame, one spirit, one light. Stay concentrated without looking away for as long as possible. Notice the background moving and changing. When the eyes begin to feel watery or tired close them and concen-

trate on the reflection of the candle flame inside the head. Again, melt into it and let it consume your self. Stay with it as long as it is still there. Even when you open your eyes you may still see it. It will seem to be moving. Try to slow it down and make it still so you can enter into it. When your candle flame has disappeared look around you. Note how different everything appears. You may see different colors and flashes of energy cross the room. Look at the air. Can you see tiny little particles of light bouncing everywhere? Look carefully. This exercise can also be done staring into the fireplace. Be sure not to sit too close to the fire.

2.   Another concentration exercise consists of concentrating on the second hand of a watch or clock as it circles around. Every time a thought enters let it flow by, don't let it carry you away from your point of concentration. Each thought is like a fishhook trying to catch you, the fish. See how long you can concentrate without getting hooked into thinking about something else. Time yourself.

3.   Concentration can be practiced on anything— on mandalas, on energy diagrams, on interesting symbols and pictures, on a tree, on a cloud, on anything. Concentrate on an object of your choice. See what is coming out of your eyes and going into that object. Close your eyes and remember all the details of the object. See its reflection inside of your closed eyes. Open your eyes and look at the object again. Go deeper and increase your ability to concentrate as you practice.

4.   Choose an object. Concentrate on it and at the same time draw all your energy up from your heart to the point between the eyebrows inside the head, joining heart and head. Send the energy out of your eyes into the object. Now expand out from your Center into the object. Put yourself inside that object. Become the whole object inside and out. Now feel your self merge or melt into it completely so there's no separation between you and it. Forget your self. You are one. Stay in this oneness, repeating the steps over and over as much as you need to stay one. Even if you

don't feel like it is happening, keep imagining it, as that will set the energies going for it to happen. There is a fine line difference between imagination and reality. They both work to create the other.

5.   Do exercise number 4 on a person. You can both do it together by looking into each other's eyes, or you can look at the other without him even knowing, such as when he is reading or sleeping. Another way to practice it in the family is to have one person sit in the middle of the circle and the others practice the exercise on that person. Each person in the center will feel different. Try to note their different vibrations. A variation is to have the person in the center look into each person's eyes in turn. Look for the same light of consciousness in each other and pouring out each other's eyes.

6.   This concentration exercise is one that can be very useful in stilling the mind any time of day and also can be practiced as you sit to meditate. What is done here is to repeat a sound mentally over and over again, and rhythmically tune it to the breath. We begin practicing it by sitting up in meditation posture as relaxed as we can be. Inhale through the nostrils slowly to a mental count of five to ten. Hold to the same count, and then exhale slowly to the same mental count. Be sure to do each part for the same count. Repeat five or ten times. When you are finished relax and let the breath go. You will feel an inner balance and your breathing will be slowed down. This exercise is very good for hyperactive children and for people with nervous tensions. Now, watch your breath as it naturally flows. Watch it as if you were watching someone else breathing. If it wants to stay in awhile, or out awhile, let it. Don't control it or force it. Just let the breath do its own thing. When you feel like you are really hearing someone else breathing inside you, mentally say the word *Sa* as the breath comes in and then *Ha* when the breath is ready to go out . . . *Sa* again as it returns in and *Ha* again as it goes out. Really relax and yet focus at the same time. Repeat for several

minutes building up the length of time you can do it as you practice. Some people enjoy this exercise for twenty to thirty minutes at a time. Many yoga disciplines use an exercise similar to this. They call the repeated word a *mantra*. Eventually the breath disappears and the sound dies away into the still Center. If the mind starts to wander, gently bring it back to the *Sa Ha* sound again and again. Remember we are training the mind to do what we want it to do, but we can't force. As with children, forcing causes the mind to rebel and just reinforces the difficulty. If the mind insists on wandering, stop for a minute and do some toning (explained in the next exercise) and then come back to this rhythmic *Sa Ha* concentration. You can also try this exercise lying down, but there is a possibility of falling asleep. On the other hand, if you have difficulty sleeping you can try this technique as a means to get to sleep.

7. Toning or Chanting. Toning primal sounds like *Aaaahhh* or *Ooommm* creates vibrations and resonances that help to still the restless mind. As the sounds build up and interact with other sounds, different sounds within sounds can be heard, like tinkling bells. These sounds produce energies that work to dissolve thought waves. So, at any time during the meditation or any time the mind starts to run away, just tone the primal sound *Oooooommmmmm* or *Aaaahhh* deep within the diaphragm.

You have to concentrate and put consciousness into the sound as you do it or it won't work. Let it dissolve your waves of thought through listening carefully to the sound at the same time you are concentrating on it. LISTEN carefully, not with your physical ears, but from your inner being. Feel it vibrating all over, in every cell in your body. Fill yourself up with the sound. Hear it vibrate in sounds around you as well. Then listen again in the stillness in between. When you are meditating in a group you will have to listen carefully as you tone in order to harmonize with the other persons' chanting so it resonates together. One person may have to lead and decide when to start and stop the chanting so there is not a lot of discordance and disruption to the meditation. Try it both ways, spontaneously and with someone leading.

Group toning or chanting can really help children to want to stay in meditation longer. It can also help the family feel closer together and united. A good feeling of group awareness comes when everyone is concentrating and listening to everyone else and not just off on their own trip.

Sometimes a guitar chord, bells or other musical instrument can be used with chanting. This can be a fun family activity as well as a concentration exercise if we really stay centered as we do it. A tremendous amount of energy can be built up and released through toning. If we direct this energy on a wave of thought toward someone who is ill or depressed, the energy can have a healing or uplifting effect on that person. It doesn't matter whether they are in the same room. Our directed thought is not limited by space.

THE MEDITATIONS

In the course of going through each of these meditations, keep referring to the centering meditation, which was described in Chapter 1 and given again here, as the beginning meditation. It is the basic meditation and will quickly relax body, feelings and thoughts. You may even want to do it first, before practicing any of the other meditations as a preparation for each session.

While leading young children in the meditations, we need to leave ourself open to tune into and receive their needs. Often we find we have to improvise to keep their attention by dramatizing with the voice. The voice should be smooth, calm, and alive, not monotone. We may at times need to spontaneously simplify some of the words. With practice we learn how to tune into the rhythm of the Now, and feel out what will keep everyone going. Be as spontaneous and free as possible. Sometimes we may need to leave some words out and add others to fit the moment. The dots

. . . interspersed in the meditations indicate a long pause and are part of the rhythm. Read the meditations very slowly, making sure it's all being absorbed.

After the meditation have a discussion on what the children wish to share from their experience. Ask the children questions. What is energy? What is being centered? What is nothingness? Don't answer questions for the children. Just keep asking and get them going on their own discussion. Let them explore, guiding the discussion so it doesn't get off track. Practice these meditations over and over again. They follow nature's patterns of rhythm and authority. There is always more depth to experience. Become inspired to add new variations as you go along.

BEGINNING MEDITATION

Sit upright in a comfortable position with the back and spine straight, yet relaxed. Close the eyes. Relax the body. Tense the left foot. Let it go. Tense the right foot. Let it go. Relax all the nerves and muscles in each part as we go along. Tense the left calf and let it go. Tense the right calf and let it go. Relax each part completely. Continue with the left thigh, then the right thigh, then the left buttocks, right buttocks, abdomen and stomach, then the left chest, right chest, left forearm and hand, right forearm and hand, left upper arm, right upper arm, left shoulder, right shoulder, neck, face, head and scalp muscles. Relax the muscles behind the eyes as well. Take a deep breath and let all the tensions of pent-up feelings go. Feel loose and limp and relaxed, yet be very aware and alert. The body is peaceful. The emotions and feelings are calm. Allow the mind to relax and keep it still. Look within, inwards and up without straining.

Imagine a point between the eyebrows inside the forehead. At this point focus all the attention and interest. Concentrate, but stay relaxed. If thoughts come in don't resist them, just let them pass through and bring the attention back to the point of concentration every time it wanders. Practice this for a few minutes. Now see if you can feel the heart beating. . . Become aware of the rhythm of the breath. Soon a very peaceful, nice feeling of being centered within the heart will come. The heart and head blend as one. Melt into the deep Center. It is here that we receive a fresh supply of energy and awareness.

LISTENING MEDITATION

Close the eyes and sit upright in meditation posture, legs crossed, back straight and hands upturned on the thighs or knees. Listen . . . very carefully to your breathing. . . In and out, listen to it slow down as you listen. . . getting slower and slower. . . Put your attention on your heart and listen to it beating inside you. . . Listen to your heart beat, see if it is slowing down too. . . Now draw energy up from your heart into your head. Look inside your forehead to the spot right between your two eyebrows inside of your head. Stare inside your head at that spot, and keep bringing your attention back to that spot if it wanders. That spot is a door to the Center of your being, to the Source of energy inside of you. That is where your awareness of yourself comes to you. Ask yourself, "What is this awareness?" . . . Now, put everything you feel or think right there and feel it send back to you a wave of deep peace, deeper than when you sleep at night. Ask yourself, "Can I stay in this peace?" . . . See if you can stay there. . . Now, come out of the Source, slowly, come out of this inner eye, back into your heart. Ask yourself, "What's happening in my heart?" Now become aware of your breath again. Watch your breath. . . and now open your eyes. Feel yourself recharged, just as if you've come out of a bath of peaceful energy.

THE FIVE SENSES MEDITATION

Before beginning ask what are the five senses? What do we use them for? How do they teach us about our world? Discuss.

Now let's meditate. Sit up properly. Let's go into the Source, in the Center within. Close the eyes. Pretend you have never seen anything before. You have never seen color, people, sun, trees, nothing . . . then close the ears with the fingers . . . bring all the sounds back into the Source within . . . imagine all the energy in your nerves that you use to feel and touch with come back into the Source. . . . Now, imagine you can't smell anything . . . and now imagine you can't taste anything . . . imagine that all of your senses have disappeared into the Source. Concentrate on the Source and disappear your very self into the Source . . . Life is rhythm, nature is rhythm, life and death, night and day, we breathe in and out, in and out. So too, in meditation we bring all the energy from our five senses back into the Source and then we let the energy flow out again into our senses which we need to use to live in the world. In and out . . . Now, let's imagine our senses returning . . . our taste, we can sense the taste of our own mouth again . . . our smell, we can smell our body and we can smell the room and other bodies . . . our touch, we can feel our bones and muscles again . . . our hearing, we can hear more and more sounds . . . We can hear our breathing. What else can we hear? Listen . . . Now last of all our sight. Let's open our eyes and look around. What is the first thing you see? Do things look different?

TRIANGLE MEDITATION

Sit up straight in meditation posture. Be sure your palms are face up and open, resting on your knees or thighs. Be very still. Concentrate deeply at the point between the eyebrows inside the head. Try to really center there. Imagine there's a magnet at that center pulling you into it, pulling your heart and all your feelings and thoughts together into that magnet . . . Now feel the center of the palm of each hand . . . feel a little tingling of energy in each palm as you connect a line of energy between your left hand and your right hand. Then, between your right hand and the Center between the brows inside the head, and between that Center in your head and the left palm. Feel energy flowing in all the three Centers, on light energy between your two hands and your head, just like a triangle. Feel the Center in your head become stronger and stronger. Look within. What do you feel? What do you see?

At another time this meditation can be done concentrating at the Center in the middle of the chest, the heart Center, as the first point of the triangle instead of the head.

HEARTBEAT MEDITATION

Sit upright in meditation posture. Concentrate on the point between the eyebrows inside the head. Imagine it is a very still, quiet spot . . . so still that it makes your breath seem like a strong wind blowing in and out. Each time you breathe in you are drawing the breeze in to that quiet Center. Each time you breathe out you are letting the breeze blow out into the whole universe . . . (long pause) . . . Now, imagine and feel your own heartbeat . . . (long pause) . . . and the heartbeat of everyone else . . . the heartbeat of the sun, and imagine all the stars having a heartbeat too. Feel the heartbeat of the whole universe in each breath. Imagine that there's one Cosmic heartbeat, in everything . . . beating like a Cosmic Drum that never stops. . . .

OM MEDITATION

Sit upright in meditation posture. Close your eyes and look within. Look at the tiny speckles of light or bursts of color. Now, keeping your eyes closed, press your thumb or forefinger against each ear to block out all sound from outside. Listen to the inner sounds. You have to be very still to hear them. Concentrate on these sounds . . . listen behind the sounds for an even deeper sound. Put your whole Self into the sound . . . softly hum the sound you hear. Then listen again in silence . . .

Now, imagine this inner sound is a motor running the entire universe. Go into it. Feel it vibrating your whole being . . . vibrating the whole universe . . . Really put yourself into it . . . Now, still listening, open your eyes and unplug your ears. Can you still hear the same sound? Listen carefully . . . Can you hear it running all the atoms in the whole universe? *Listen.* Hum *Ooooommmm* to it. *Oooommmm . . . Oooommmm.* See if you can stay with it all day long and even when you're lying in bed at night.

Now, let's lie down in a circle with our heads touching in

the center, like the hub of a wheel. Let's listen for the Om sound again and start to chant Om softly, when you hear it. *Oooommmm, Oooommmm.* Feel it vibrating in each others' heads like electricity. *Ooommmm.* Feel all your cells vibrating with the sound. Stay with the resonance and the stillness afterwards.

CHANTING MEDITATION

(A good meditation to do right before the mirroring exercise on page 141.) Sit in meditation posture and close the eyes. As we chant let's see if we can listen to the ear of the ear . . . the inner ear that hears what the ear sends to us. Let's be aware that the One is doing the same thing in its other selves in the group. Get into that same ear of the ear, that same space which is in each of the others as well as in ourself. Feel the unity of that One playing through you and the others. Listen to that One until you experience the group as One Self, One Body, One Instrument. Let's chant. *Ooooommmm. Oooommmm.* (Chant spontaneously for awhile, listening carefully all the time . . . .) Now listen in the stillness . . . staying in the One, in that deep Center of being, know that as you open your eyes that same One will be looking through them through the eye of the eye, just as it did through the ear of the ear. And that One will be seeing Itself in the others and looking out of the others' eyes too.

THE CIRCLE AND DOT MEDITATION

Sit up straight and be very still, without moving a muscle. Concentrate on the Center between the eyebrows inside your head. Look into the center and see a dot with a circle. You are the dot and the circle is the world . . . see what color your dot is and see what color your circle is. (Go very slowly, keeping your rhythm attuned to the children . . .)

Very still . . . very quiet . . . Now, put Love in your dot
with you; and as you love, your dot gets bigger, and the
more you love with your heart, the bigger the dot . . . feel
love flowing from your heart into your dot . . . the more
you love the bigger the dot . . . and it gets bigger and bigger
and bigger, still very quiet, and bigger and bigger and bigger, still very quiet, and bigger and bigger until all of a
sudden the dot and the circle are one. You and the whole
world are One . . . (pause for as long as the child is
still . . .) What color was your dot? What color was your
circle? And now what color did it all become? The more
love the bigger it got. Did you know that the circle is really
many more dots just like yours? All the people in the world
are like dots making up the world which is the circle.

WE ARE ONE MEDITATION

(A good group meditation for before group awareness sessions. Go very slowly.) Sit in meditation posture. Concentrate on the point between the eyebrows inside the head.
Stay in that center as you draw energy up from the heart
and bring it into that point between the eyebrows. Keep
drawing the energy up from your heart to the center between the eyes behind the forehead. Now imagine a point in
the center of the group circle, and send energy from the
point between the eyebrows to that point in the center of
the circle. Now expand yourself from that point to include
the whole circle and everyone in it. Feel yourself become
the whole circle and become everyone. Melt into it until
you are it, and feel the Oneness. Let's all chant
Oooommmm in the Oneness. *Oooommmmmm*.

YOU ARE LIGHT

Lie down flat on the back in this meditation. Arms to the
sides, palms up in The Corpse posture. Feel your toes.

Imagine that your toes are disappearing, vanishing into atoms into the air. Feel your feet. Feel them disappear into the light around. No feet, only light. Feel your ankles and feel them disappear. Now your legs are vanishing. Feel your knees and feel them disappear, dissolve into light. Imagine your buttocks and stomach disappear into light, dissolved in the air. Feel your chest and feel it totally disappear. And now the arms . . . they're so light they are disappearing. Feel your shoulders and feel them disappear into light. Feel your chin and feel it dissolve— into the atoms, electrons, protons, neutrons, photons of light from which it is made. And now imagine your mouth and cheeks and nose dissolve into pure energy, into light. Your eyes and forehead are disappearing and now the very top of your head has disappeared into light . . . there is no body left, it has entirely disappeared into energy. All of its atoms have dissolved into pure energy— light— nothing. Now dissolve your thought waves into pure energy too. There is nothing left, just your real self. Nothing left but your awareness . . . that came to earth when you were born, to live, work, play and grow in your body. But you have forgotten who you really are. You began to believe you were your body. Now do you remember what it's like to have no body? No thoughts? Who are you?

THE WELL

Form your hands into fists and gently tap your head all over commanding your brain cells to wake up. Sit up and close your eyes, going straight within to the Center. Let's dip into the Source like we are dipping a pail into a well and drawing forth light energy as if we are drawing forth water from the well . . . Now, pour that energy from the Source all through each part of the body to wash it with light and fresh awareness, fresh consciousness. Pour it through the head, chest, arms, trunk, buttocks, legs, feet. Wash the body with light inside-out.

GRASS MEDITATION

On a sunny day go outdoors and sit comfortably, relaxing, just looking at the grass. Imagine yourself becoming the grass. Feel grassness. Experience yourself moving in the wind. The grass seems brighter, more alive, fresh and new . . . Feel your greenness— sparkly and light— and maybe there is some feeling of coolness or wetness, even though the sun is shining. Commune with the life in the grass. Experience its purity. Experience its oneness with the life in yourself. Stay with this until it is real for you.

MANDALA MEDITATION

Pin the mandala shown in the back of the book on a wall and sit about three to four feet away from it. Look at the black and white symbol carefully. Now close your eyes and press your fingers on your closed eyelids, gently pushing against your eyeballs for a minute or so. What do you see? Do you see the same symbol— the black and white checkerboard energy pattern moving inside? Now, sit upright in meditation posture and concentrate with your heart and mind on the center of the mandala. Really put all of your attention on that central spot. Feel like you are being drawn into that center like diving into a lake of white energy . . . . Don't let your concentration wander . . . . Now that you are in the center, begin to expand yourself out from the center to the whole mandala. See the spirals of energy form like flower petals. Now look back into the center again, bringing the whole mandala back into the center with you. Do you see the spirals spinning one way, then the other? What colors do you see? Keep looking. Do you see sparkles of white light coming off the paper? Let them flow in and out of you. Imagine that you are marching down a long tunnel into the center. You are marching straight into and now right through the center, and coming out the other side into pure light— total openness. Your whole being is in this open light. Feel like you are this light energy, pure consciousness.

PROTECTION MEDITATION

Sometimes children and adults will have frightening experiences in meditation. We may see monsters or devils, just as we do in dreams or nightmares. But in meditation, unlike a nightmare, we are conscious and can always change our consciousness. We need to understand that we can protect ourself from ourself. Monsters or devils are part of our consciousness, some things we've been told are out to get us, just as angels are part of our consciousness too. When anything scary starts to happen we can quickly use our will to say I am Master of myself. Out devil, out monster. We can do this in meditation to wash away all the fear and negative energy and replace it with love, light and bliss. Sometimes people send us bad vibes and we can protect ourself from them with this meditation too.

If you ever feel scared that there are bad vibes, monsters or evil forces attacking you, immediately call on your higher Self, your white knight in shining armor. Close your eyes and be still. Imagine a beautiful white light coming through the top of your head like a gushing waterfall and imagine it fill up your whole body. Feel the white light pour into your face, your eyes, ears, nose and mouth. Feel it bubble down into your neck and chest and down your arms and hands. Now, imagine it filling up your heart with peaceful, blissful white light, so light and blissful . . . It's flowing into your stomach, calm and light, then down through your buttocks and your thighs, knees, calves, feet and out through your toes. Feel as though you've turned into a white light waterfall. Feel the freshness of its energy gushing in and through and all around you, cleansing you of any fearful thoughts or feelings, protecting you like a shield, loving you with its sweet, soothing light. Every cell of your body is filled with this light. Stay in this peace for awhile.

Realize you are master of your consciousness and you can change anything into love and light with your imagination and will. Your imagination and will are like an angel with a magic wand ready to serve you.

SPACESHIP MEDITATION

Imagine there is a spaceship inside of your head. Step inside your spaceship, right in the center of your head. See what color it is. Feel it take off and go all the way through the top of your head, up, up, up, past millions of planets and stars on its way . . . up, up, up . . . keep going up, forever . . . observe what you see . . . now go all the way down in your spaceship . . . down, down, down . . . down, down through the center of the earth and out the other side, down, down, down . . . forever . . . down . . . Now go up again, up, up, up . . . all the way up, higher and farther this time, up, up, up . . . now go all the way to the left . . . farther and farther . . . forever to the left . . . now all the way to the right . . . farther, farther, farther, farther . . . look around at what you see . . . Now come back to center space station and go all the way forward, straight in front, straight on, farther, farther, farther . . . What do you hear? . . . farther . . . and now go all the way back, behind, back, back, farther back, on and on, farther and farther, back, back . . . . Now, come back slowly to the center . . . come back into the top of your head and now you are inside your head again. Step out of your spaceship. You have traveled over and through the entire universe. You are the light of the entire universe . . . Open your eyes, look around your little universe here. What did you see in your universe? Meditate on the whole universe as something you experience inside your own awareness, inside your own consciousness . . .

JOURNEY THROUGH INNERSPACE

Concentrate at the center between the eyebrows inside the head. This is the spiritual eye. Stare at it for a little bit, being perfectly quiet. Now move your awareness to the very top of your head, at the center top of your brain. Feel a lightness and imagine a funnel of energy, like a white tornado, coming in the top of your head. Feel the two centers connect, the one between the eyebrows and the one on top of the head. Feel like you are taking a blissful brain bath in the energy . . . Now move your awareness to the back of your neck and the energy flowing in there too . . . move down to your heart center and feel all the other centers come together in the heart center, the center of our love. Feel them all become one center. The center between your eyebrows, the top of your head, the back of your neck and your heart all become One . . . Now let's chant the sound Om through our heart on a wave of love to fill the whole universe with music, with love. *Ooooooommmmmmmmmm Ooooommmmm* . . . Listen in the still silence . . . feel the energy flow on into your stomach and then into the very bottom of your spine. Imagine that we are bringing all this energy back down to earth and grounding it here on the earth, ready to go into whatever activity we are going to do. Stop. What needs to be done next? Think. How are you going to do it? Open your eyes and share what it is you want to do. If okay, then do it . . .

EVERYTHING IS HAPPENING INSIDE OF YOU

Close your eyes and sit up in meditation posture. Breathe in the air deeply through your nose. Feel your nose smelling. What tells you that you are smelling? . . . Your brain receives the messages from the nerves in your nose . . . What tells you what you are hearing? . . . Your brain receives the messages from the ears . . . Now taste the taste in your own mouth . . . What is telling you about the taste? . . . Your brain receives the messages from your tongue . . . Now feel your body inside and feel the air on it outside . . . What tells you what you are feeling? . . . The brain . . . Now, don't move . . . open your eyes. Without moving anything but your eyes, look around. What's telling you that you are seeing? Your brain receives the messages the eyes send to it. Your brain is like a huge messenger— a huge telephone exchange— who's on the other end of the phone? Who does the brain send its messages to? Who does it tell? YOU . . . Can you imagine or think of anything that you don't experience inside your own consciousness, inside your head? Everything is within you. Stars, sun, space, the universe is all within you.

GRAVITATION AND RADIATION MEDITATION

(Go very slowly) Sitting in meditation posture, very quietly, concentrate at the point between the eyebrows inside the head. Draw your self into the center of the head, deep inside the brain. Look carefully. Feel and see waves and flashes of light, energy, coming into the center. Step back inside your head. Imagine and feel like you are pulling everything, including everything you are hearing, seeing, touching, tasting, smelling, thinking, dreaming, imagining, all the stars, light and sound, all thoughts, feelings, everything into this center where your Self is sitting . . . A black hole drawing all like gravity into itself . . . Stay with this for awhile, drawing everything in, feeling very deep. Your self is empty and full at the same time . . . When you've drawn in all you can, be still and experience your fullness . . .

Now we're going to send everything back out again . . . Begin to send energy back out from this still center, out, out, out, beyond the walls of your head, out into the air, filling the whole room with energy . . . through the walls of the room and house into the sky . . . the trees . . . the city . . . the whole earth . . . Imagine and feel yourself like the sun, radiating energy out like light into the oceans, the mountains, the fields. Keep expanding, sending everything back out of you . . . and now you are in outer space watching the earth get farther and farther away . . . You keep expanding and expanding, beyond the sun and milky way until there's nothing left in you. You feel so light and floating, you feel like you are nothing you are so light. Now you are in pure space— beyond the stars . . . . being pure nothing. Nothing and everything, dark and light. It's all your Self.

ALL IS ENERGY

Close your eyes and become very still in meditation . . . very still, like you are stopping the world . . . Now imagine that movement is just beginning inside you. Everything you see inside of you is energy whirling . . . Imagine that all the different things in the room are made of energy, tiny atoms of energy . . . Imagine that each of the cells in your body is made of energy and is drinking in energy . . . Imagine your feelings as energy moving around inside you, and all your thoughts are made of waves of energy, and everything you can imagine is energy . . . Now when you open your eyes look straight ahead. Can you see tiny bits of energy bouncing into each other as you look through the air? Zillions of bits of energy? . . Look at someone else's eyes . . . do you see light twinkling in their eyes? That's energy. Look around the room . . . See if you can see energy and light coming from everything in the room, everywhere . . . What lights up the energy you see? . . Is it the energy itself inside everything? . . Is it the sun? . . . . Is it the light of your own Self coming out of your eyes? . . Is it all of these? . . .

ENERGY FOLLOWS THOUGHT

Think of something you'd like to change in yourself. Some improvement you'd like to make. Decide what it is going to be before going into meditation. Perhaps you'd like more willpower, to be more loving, more helpful or a better reader, a mathematical wizard, lose ten pounds, stop smoking, etc. Decide what it is you need . . . Meditation can give you a boost to make it occur. Close your eyes and become as relaxed as possible. Sit in meditation and relax every muscle as you learned in the beginning meditation. Feel your whole body become so relaxed, from the toes to the top of the head, that you no longer even feel it. You are somewhere else. Relax all your emotions and feelings . . . let them float away . . . so there's nothing but peace left . . . Become so relaxed that your thoughts are drifting away and you are just floating on a flying carpet, sailing in empty space . . .

Now, in this empty stillness we are going to place a new thought . . . Put in just the thought of what you decided you would like to change. Imagine yourself already in this new change. Picture what you'd be like. See yourself already there, already changed . . . Imagine the new you . . . Realize you have set powerful energy moving to make your desire happen. Don't let any other thought in, especially no doubts. Keep repeating this exercise over and over so you will reinforce the new pattern and when it becomes stronger than the old one it will come true . . . But remember, only choose something that won't hurt you or anyone else. Whatever you send to another bounces back to yourself like a ball bounces, because there is only one energy, one Source, one Self. Now when you have completed your imagining and can feel the new change in your being, count to three and come back into your body and open your eyes. 1 . . . 2 . . . 3 . . .

After this meditation demonstrate how Newton's law works— that every action has an equal and opposite reaction. Bounce a ball or use some other method to show your children and yourself how this energy works. The same law operates with our thoughts and feelings toward others.

This meditation can be modified by taking only one person's new change at a time and the whole group can meditate on it with that person. Everyone imagine the person as changed and add energy to the change. This way we can participate in each other's changes more and help them. We can also do this meditation just before falling asleep at night. Instead of putting in a self-suggestion for change, we put in a positive thought that we will receive a solution to some problem that is troubling us. We program a solution or answer to come during our sleep or the next day. Then we sleep on it and give the unconscious an opportunity to deliver the results either in a dream or shortly after we wake up.

Chapter 7

Evolutionary Awareness Exercises

These awareness exercises include many different types of individual, person-to-person and group interactions. They are all for the purpose of getting in touch with real feelings and communicating them, expanding consciousness and experiencing deeper love and joy with others. They can be expanded out of the family for use in schools, after-school activities and as games for children and adults to enjoy with friends.

As we progress through practicing the meditations and awareness exercises we discover we are learning about each other from the inside-out, from the inner being outwards. The closer to the center we are, the clearer we will see, the fewer the filters. Remember, all is seen through each person's own consciousness. The real nature of our relationships with our children regarding authority, discipline, respect, trust and open sharing are reflected back to us in these sessions. Expect to see this reflection. Look for it. Like a movie, it will tell us about ourself and about our family situation. Everyone will be reflecting each other's attitudes back to them. Commitment to keep on with the sessions is important for real, meaningful changes to unfold.

Do all of the exercises and then repeat the ones you find work the best again and again. There is always more to explore. Children who practice these exercises will naturally learn how to overcome self-centeredness and to redirect energy into constructive outlets.

There are seven basic levels of awareness in human beings. These levels are briefly discussed in Chapter 2. We mentioned that we all have all the levels within us as they interlock and work together. Usually we have one or two that dominate and strongly color the way we relate to the world. One of the biggest causes for misunderstanding between people is that we don't understand where the other is coming from. We don't really know how or why they think the way they do. Why does Thelma always talk about the future? Why does Douglas always talk about sex, food and money and wife Jeanne always talk about when the kids were little and the funny things they used to do, just like she used to do when she and her sisters were little? It is because each of these people have different drives and live on different levels. Each level is like a world unto itself and offers a different type or quality of love. (See chart on page 9 .)

Communication between people coming from these different inner-worlds doesn't usually connect. Usually we just talk at each other unless we are able to get inside others and experience their world with them. Otherwise we may hear someone say something from their level and they will mean something different by it than how we interpret it from our own level. There is a popular saying that tells the story very well: "I know that you believe you understand what you think I said, but I am not sure you realize that what you heard is not what I meant."

Many of the following exercises are to help us learn to really be with others, inside their worlds. They are to help us gain some experience of sharing love and communing at all seven levels.

EXERCISES FOR SEVEN LEVELS OF SHARING

Imaginative—Violet

1.   Make Believe. The entire family plays make-believe together. Each decides what kind of a character they will be and then we clear the room for a stage and act it out spontaneously. Everyone being as free as they can in their role.

2.   Drama. One child is the director and assigns the roles each person is to play. The children can rotate being director. Maybe Mom will be the baby and Susy the Mom. Whatever the director wants, that's who the others are for that time. Each person must really put their whole self into the role to make it as real as possible.

3.   Psychodrama. Each person becomes someone else in the family, and acts out that person as best they can. Choose a scene, for example, eating dinner, and everybody switch roles and eat like the person whose role they are playing.

4.   Tell Me A Story! We all tell the story together. One. person starts, then the next person takes over to continue the tale, and so on, until the story is brought to an end. Be as wild and as imaginative as you can. Tape record it if possible. Is there a meaning to the story? Is each person's personality expressed?

(These next exercises for communing on the imaginative level are to help develop the will along with it, so that the imagination can serve us better.)

5.   Mannequin. Close your eyes. Imagine that you are going to take your body apart. First you remove your feet and put them on the ground right next to you . . . Then remove your legs and fit them as they belong, on top of the feet . . . Now, remove your trunk, the stomach and chest and buttocks, and put it on top of the legs . . . Now take the arms and put them where they go on the trunk. Fit them

on . . . And now, put the head and neck on the trunk. Be sure to get it on straight. Now your body is next to you and you are left. Ask yourself, Who am I? . . . Who am I? . . . Now, we are going to bring our body back. Bring back your head and neck. Then bring back your arms, then the trunk with the chest, stomach and buttocks . . . fit your legs back on the trunk, then the feet. Now you are all back together again. Open your eyes. (You may want to blindfold everyone if some of the young children have difficulty keeping their eyes closed.)

6. Scrying. In scrying we distract the mind and allow the imagination to express itself. Sit before a mirror. Sit comfortably and relax completely. Look at the mirror. Look behind its surface into its depth. Really get to know it. Look all over it. What does a mirror do? . . . Imagine the surface of the mirror is colored. Gaze at the mirror's surface, holding the image of the color in your mind. Watch for it to actually appear on the mirror. Once you've been able to see color, image something simple, like a tree or a wagon, etc. Then practice projecting animals, then humans. Be sure to hold and control the image you want to see and refuse any other pictures that pop into your imagination. You will learn about the power of the imagination to project images and beliefs onto the mirror of life through practicing this exercise. You have to be relaxed for good results.

7. Brain Expansion Exercise. Everyone sit facing the same direction. Close your eyes. Imagine you are sitting in the middle of the room and the room is a big box. Imagine that each corner of this box has a magnet in it. There are eight corners, four corners on the top where the ceiling and walls meet and four on the bottom where the floor and the walls meet. There you are, sitting, right in the middle. Now, imagine your mind has grown and has wrapped itself around the box so the box is inside your mind and you are sitting inside your mind too. With the eyes closed take a deep breath and blow the breath all out and mentally send it to the front top left corner of the box. Feel the breath fasten

onto the magnet. Feel the magnet pull at your brain like it is pulling the brain into itself. Let the breath come back in by itself and then blow it out again to the front, top, left corner of the box. Feel that magnet tugging at your brain cells, stretching your brain. Now blow out once more to the front, top, left corner . . . This time when the breath comes in we're going to blow out to the front, top, right corner, feel the magnet pull at our brain cells, waking them up. Now blow out again to that front, top, right corner. Feel your brain growing. And once more to that corner. Then proceed to the back, top, right corner and blow out, feeling the back of the brain stretch in the same way. Do it three times to this corner. Then to the back, top, left corner and repeat three times. Be sure to feel the magnet pulling. Then do the bottom four corners just as you did the top four. One person can repeat the instructions directing everyone into the proper corners, until everyone has learned the exercise by heart. Begin to feel the walls disappear. Feel like the magnets are stars, centers of light energy, pulling your brain cells which are also stars— and you are sitting at the center of the entire universe.

8. Beginning Gestalt Dream Interpretation. Take a dream, or a part of a dream if you can't remember it all, and describe it to another person. The other person writes down the main points and the characters as they are told. Then go back to the beginning of the description and describe the dream again, only this time you are going to be all the parts of the dream. For example, if there was a room in the dream become the room and say, "I am a dark room, I am green and there are spider webs in my corners." If there is a clock in the dream describe yourself as the clock. Become the clock. How does it feel? "I tick loudly and I don't run on time." Become each person in the dream in the same way. Always speak using the word "I." If there is a hairy monster in the dream say, "I am a hairy monster" and describe what you are like. If your mother is in the dream, that's part of you too and you describe your mother saying, "I am

_____." The other person writes down all of these different parts just as they are described.

After these two descriptions are completed go over what has been written in the "I" part all at once. Ask yourself if there is a part of you like all the parts in your dream. For example, "I am green and I have spider webs in my corners. I am also a clock and I tick loudly and don't run on time" . . . and so forth. String them all together to get the picture. Is there a part of you that is green (neutral, new, sickly, whatever green means to you)? Is there a part of you that hasn't been cared for and is dusty with spider webs? Is there a part of you that makes loud noises but doesn't run on time (gets to places late, doesn't eat or sleep regularly)? Don't skip any object or person in the dream. The idea is that they are all parts of your self. Your dreams are all a projection of your consciousness, what is going on in you. Can you see how life is a dream too?

9. War on Disease. When we are ill the body fights the infection, the virus, whatever the foreign invader is, by attacking it with the body's white blood cells as soldiers. These blood cells are called white corpuscles or phagocytes. When we have a cold these phagocytes attack the bacillus cold germ until they are destroyed. So, when we are sick we do a meditation to help the process. We center and do some deep breathing. Inhale to a count of five, hold to a count of five, exhale to a count of five. Repeat ten times. Then we imagine those phagocytes armed with swords and tanks killing the bacteria and washing it out of the body. We imagine that we are sending fresh supplies of energy and ammunition to the phagocytes by taking good care of ourself, by drinking lots of liquids, by getting lots of rest and by vividly visualizing the phagocytes winning the war. We tune into the Source of all energy and life in meditation and see the phagocytes take over the bacteria and win the war. We help to heal ourself.

Intuition—Indigo (Dark Blue)

Sharing love intuitively is an experience that goes beyond words into direct knowing. We can experience telepathy (reading what is in another's mind), we can read auras (seeing the color surrounding a person which shows his level of awareness at that time), we can have many unusual experiences called psychic, or ESP. (extra-sensory perception). These experiences are unusual, of course, until they become usual, for we want to develop this intuitive level.

1.   The intuitive eye.

One person, the leader, takes a flat tray and without showing anyone, puts ten different household objects on the platter, like a pen, spoon, pliers, soap, etc. Make sure the objects can be seen on the tray. Cover the tray with a towel. Bring the covered tray into the room where everyone else is waiting. Everyone who can write should have a paper and pencil. Do a meditation to tune in. At the end of the meditation everyone tries to see with the intuitive eye what is on the covered tray and writes their guesses down. Then the leader removes the towel for one minute and everyone looks at the tray trying to remember everything on it. After one minute the towel is put back on and everyone writes down what they remember on the other side of the paper. After a few minutes more, lift off the towel and compare. How good was your intuitive eye? How good was your memory?

2.   Telepathy exercises.

a.   One person sits in front of another. One holds the wrists of the other. The one to receive is the one who holds the wrists and the one who broadcasts is the one who is having his wrists held. Pretend that the receiver is a transistor radio and the broadcaster is the radio station on the other side of town, sending out the radio waves. The broadcaster sends a message mentally of just a few words. The receiver keeps his mind blank and tunes in to the broadcaster. He really listens inwardly to get the right station. Then he plays back whatever he picks up. Then switch roles. One person may be a better sender than receiver and vice versa. With practice success will come.

  b. One person goes out of the room. The others decide what they will have him do when he walks back in, for example, hop on one foot. They will then all close their eyes and vividly imagine and see him hopping on one foot. They hold a picture of him doing this in their imagination and send the image and thought to him as he comes into the room. He tunes in and does whatever comes to him. Each person takes a turn.

  c. Everyone lines up with their backs to the leader. The leader chooses one from the line and stares at him without his knowing it. He sends him a message and energy. Whoever feels the energy or the message does what he feels he is being told. After awhile turn around to see if it is you. The leader tells everyone who it was for and what the message was. Take turns.

(All three of these telepathy exercises need practice to get used to the new mode of communication.)

  d. One person is blindfolded. Everyone else lines up in any random order. One by one everyone stands in front of the blindfolded person. The blindfolded person holds out his hands to pick up the vibration of that person but may not physically touch that person. He guesses who it is. Without saying yes or no the person moves to the end of the line and the next person moves in front of the blindfolded person. After everyone has stood in front of him, then the blindfolded person may take his blindfold off. Tell him how many he guessed correctly. Take turns being blindfolded. Practice this exercise repeatedly at other times until everyone is familiar with everyone else's vibrations when they are blindfolded.

3.   Dowsing.

Make pendulums for everyone. Use a white or black string. Tie the string to a small object that is black or white or green— a spool of thread, a small black ball with a pin stuck in it for the thread to tie around, or large round buttons make good beginning pendulums. Provide each person with a bar magnet, or take turns if there is only one magnet. Point the positive end south and the negative end to the north like a compass.

Hold the string of the pendulum between the thumb and forefinger, pointing them downwards, and place them over the north pole of the magnet. After a few moments the pendulum will start to respond to the magnet's field and by itself will begin to rotate in one direction. Let it rotate for a minute or two then move the pendulum to the south pole of the magnet. What happened? The pendulum should have reversed its rotation to the opposite direction. Tie the pendulum to a solid object above the north pole of the magnet so you are not holding it. It doesn't rotate. Why? Because it is your consciousness interacting with the magnetic field unconsciously through your nervous system that causes the rotation.

Take a penny and without looking to see if it is heads or tails put it under a piece of paper. Tell your consciousness that if the penny is heads the pendulum will rotate clockwise, to the right, and if the penny is tails it will rotate counterclockwise, to the left. Now, place your pendulum over the paper that the penny is under and watch the pendulum obey your command and tell you whether the penny is heads or tails. If you keep getting the opposite answer each time you toss the penny, ask yourself which way is heads? Which way is tails? See what the pendulum does. Let it tell you what the rotation means, what code it wants.

Agree on an object to hide. Now everyone but one person leave the room with their pendulums. One person hide the object. The others come back in. Ask the pendulum which way is yes? Which way is no? Then when you've found your own code, ask it if the object is on this side of the room, yes or no? Let it respond. Keep asking it yes or no questions until you find the object. Anytime you lose something you can use a pendulum to help you find it. You will have greater success if you can use a witness, which means you hold another object, just like the one you lost, in your hand as you search. For example, if you lost a shoe, hold the other shoe in your hand.

4.   Triangulation.

One person takes off his own sock or another article of his own clothing. That person leaves the room while someone else hides it. Then the person comes back in and stands in the middle of the room. If you are the one, hold out your hand, fingers out and turn in a circle, eyes closed, and try to tune in to your own missing piece of clothing. It has your vibrations on it. When you feel a tingle open your eyes and walk in the direction your hand is pointing. Then tune in again. Close the eyes and turn in a circle and see if you feel the tingle. Open your eyes and walk in that direction a few feet. Then tune in one more time. Stop, close your eyes and turn around until you feel some response in your hand, open your eyes and walk in that direction. By now you may have zeroed in on the area. Follow where you feel it is. The others can help now by saying hot or cold. Practice this exercise until you can tune in to objects successfully.

5.   Feeling colors.

Cut seven different colored pieces of paper to the same size. Try for bright colors of the spectrum: red, orange, yellow, green, blue, indigo and violet. You can use white or black if you don't have one of the spectral colors. One person at a time is blindfolded. The papers are mixed up and laid out in front of the blindfolded person who holds his hands over the pieces of paper to pick up the vibrations and the warmness or coldness coming from the paper. Then he tries to guess the colors. Someone records what he got correct and incorrect. Then the next person is blindfolded and so on. (In one high school class I taught, three girls got 100 percent correct. To their surprise, they said each paper felt so different and "told" them what color it was.) You can use four pieces of paper to learn with instead of seven if you find it a difficult exercise. Everyone feels the different vibrations, but we don't usually know what colors to associate them with until we become familiar with them. So practice.

6.   How to see auras.

Sit in a partially lit room in the evening. Have one person sit in front of a white or light colored background. Look at that person, look around their head. Can you see any colors coming from the head or face? Hold your two forefingers in front of your eyes, horizontally, with the tips touching. Bring them back and forth at different distances in front of your eyes until you see a sausage form in between the two fingers. That's where your eyes are slightly disfocused. Look beyond the sausage at the person. With your eyes slightly out of focus see if you can see any colors coming off the face or around the head. Practice this with different lighting until you see something. Research has shown that eighty percent of adults can see auras if they learn how to adjust their eyes. You can also use the pendulum to ask what a person's main aura color is. Ask, is it blue? Yes or no? Is it green? And so on.

7.   Seeing ourself in the other.

Pair off and sit knee to knee. Do a meditation in this position. When the meditation is over and you are Centered, look into each other's eyes. Send love into each other as you look. Keep looking until the eyes start to water. Look beyond the person into the soul, into the essence within. Really open yourself to receive the essence of the other. Relax. Experience your own Center, the other's Center, and experience the One, the Source that is in you and in the other. See your Self in the other, beyond the filter mirrors. See the Self reflected back to you. Stay with it, sharing and flowing into oneness. Then close your eyes. Chant *Oooommmmm*, sending yourself into the other. *Ooooommmm*. *Ooooommmmm*. Stay in the peace until you are ready to come out. (Practice this with everyone else in your family too.)

8.   Feeling sound.

One person sounds the *Oooommmmm* while the others stand in front of him holding their hands out towards him. Receive the *Oooommmmm* sound through the palms, feel it tingle or vibrate the palm.

Mind, Concepts, Memory—Blue

1.   Go around the circle and each person share the happiest, most joyful memories they can remember. Discuss them. Then go around again and each person share the most painful memory, maybe the scariest and most awful experience they can remember. Discuss.

2.   What was the first thought you had when you woke up this morning? What was the last thought you remember before falling asleep last night? Do you remember what you ate for your last breakfast? last lunch? last dinner?

3.   The next time you meditate together, when you finally get to the deepest, quietest part, someone say: Now, let's go back in time to before you were born. . . . You are now just getting ready to come into this world. Imagine yourself being born. What does it feel like? Can you remember before you were born? Being born? Discuss your thoughts with each other.

4.   Hero meditation. Most children and many adults have heroes, some person with special qualities they also would like to have. Children often imitate their heroes, trying to be like them, because children learn best through imitation. In this exercise, first do one of the centering

meditations. Then, with eyes closed, picture the person you'd like to be like. See them vividly in the mind's eye, as many details of their face and body as possible. Then visualize their good qualities and identify yourself with them (maybe it's their love, their intelligence, their talent, whatever you like). We imagine and feel those qualities are for us too. They are of the One, and since we are of the One too, those qualities are ours to have as well.

5. What I want to be. Each person describes the kind of person he would like to become. We can select someone from history or some star if we can't describe it ourself. Then the person asks the others if they think the qualities are there to become that person. If not, what needs to be strengthened, what is missing? How do others see us? How do they see our roles? Discuss. Then go on to the next person. Do the same thing until everyone has participated.

Heart, Vital Energy-Security—Green

1. Trust exercises. Everyone stand close together in a circle, the big people alternate with the little ones. One person stands in the middle, and keeping the backs of the legs straight, closes his eyes and allows himself to fall. The people in the circle catch the one in the center and then pass him to and fro to each other, caring for him, making sure he doesn't fall. This requires concentration and energy. Put love into your hands as you gently send the person (who is trusting you) to be caught by someone else in the circle. Let everyone take a turn. (If your family is made up of many small children and you are a big parent, of course you won't be able to be in the center in this exercise until you find other big people.)

Another trust exercise is for someone to lie down on the floor in The Corpse pose and become very relaxed. Everyone else stand around him. At a signal from the biggest person, everyone picks the person up and raises them as high as they can, walking a few paces. The person is relaxed, trusting, flying in the air, as everyone supports him. (Here again, big people need big supports, and only those whose weight the group can handle should be supported.)

2.   Channeling energy.

a.   Everyone sit in a circle. Hold your hands about four inches apart, palms facing each other. Push them close, then away, then close to each other without touching, as if you were squeezing an accordian. Feel the waves of air moving between the palms. Now, turn the hands so the right hand is about four inches above the left hand, palms facing each other. Close your eyes and send energy from the right palm into the left palm. Will and imagine the energy flowing into the left palm until you feel it. It may become warm or cool, it may feel tingly or tickly. Now change hands and put the left hand on top and the right hand below. Send energy; will and imagine it flowing from the left palm into the right palm. Do this until you feel it flowing. What does it feel like? Now pair off and have one person hold his hands palms up on his lap while the other person holds his hands palms down over the two hands of the first person. The person with hands palms down imagines, wills and sends energy flowing into the hands of the first person until the first person feels the energy coming in. Then they switch roles.

b.   One person sits in the middle of the circle in meditation posture, the others gather very close to him, sitting up straight. The others hold out their right hand, close their eyes and send energy out the right palm and into the heart center of the person in the middle. Imagine the energy flowing into the top of the head through the heart and out the arm into the heart of the person in the center. The person in the center just relaxes and opens up to receive the love energy coming into his heart. Keep the energy flowing until the person in the center feels it flowing in, warming him up.

Then switch to another person in the center until everyone has had a turn. If your arm gets tired, switch arms. Keep the imaging and visualizing going. Energy won't flow out your hand unless you send it out, which means concentrating. So don't let the mind wander.

c.   Everyone rub their palms together and send energy into the palms. Then hold the hands up, palms facing away, and chant *Ooooommmm* as you concentrate and send energy from your hands and voice. Direct the energy in your mind to someone you know who is in need of love, or is sick and in need of healing energy.

d.   We can help simple cuts and bruises to heal with energy. By sending energy through the palm of our hand into the hurt in another or in ourself we can help it heal. But be sure not to stop other methods of doctoring. Use channeling along with them, not as a substitute.

e.   We can channel energy to plants and animals as well as people. Plants are very sensitive and will grow much healthier if we give them love through talking to them, chanting to them and channeling energy to them. Try an experiment to prove this. Plant seeds in two pots. Use the same type of seed, dirt, pot and water. Place them both in the same amount of sunlight and give them the same amount of water. Every day, channel love energy and chant Oooommmm to one of the pots and make sure none reaches the other pot. After a few week's time see if one grows bigger and healthier than the other.

f.   Bring in a rock to the meditation circle. Put the rock in the center of the circle. Everyone meditate on the rock, try to feel its nature. What does it feel like? Become the rock; Are you hard? Porous? Still? Cold? Hot? Full of moving atoms? What are you like? What is rockness? Describe it . . . Then bring in a flower or a plant and put it in the center of the circle and take the rock away. Meditate on the plant, feeling its nature. Become the plant. Feel yourself change into it. What does it feel like? Soft? Wet? Cool?

Light? Sweet? Describe it. Can you feel the water going up your stem and into your leaves? Can you feel the cells of the plant? . . . Then take away the plant and replace it with an animal. This can be a snail, a worm, a pet animal, anything that won't run or fly away. Become it. What does it feel like? Is it scared? Happy? Warm? Hungry? Now start channeling to the animal like you did with a person. Send energy into it. Feel it, drink it in, although it might initially be afraid. Soon it will relax.

If you can find a snail, watch to see its antennae come out and move toward your hands as you channel. Snails like to drink in the energy, and they search out its source with their feelers. Experiment with other animals. They are very sensitive. When my friend's pet dog was going to have a litter of puppies she was in a lot of pain. She had accidentally mated with a male dog twice her size and she was huge. She came to us whining and pleading. We channeled to her for awhile and sent energy as we occasionally massaged her tummy. We could feel the energy going into her. It felt like a sponge soaking it up. She was in bliss, lying on her back, eyes half closed, legs sprawled for an hour as we sent energy and love. The next morning she had her twelve puppies and was fine.

Many of the great miracles that have been reported down the ages were done through great saints and wise men who have learned how to consciously direct and control vital energy or life-force. Christ and many yoga masters are known for their miracles. What is a miracle? It is really some kind of occurrence that we just don't understand how it could happen. It isn't ordinary. But through expanding our consciousness we can gain awareness of how miracles do happen and even begin to be able to direct the life-force ourself. Then they are no longer miracles to us. Luther Burbank was able to convince his roses and cacti to grow without thorns by talking to them and by sending love and energy, telling them they no longer needed their thorns to protect them. To most of us this is a miracle. Many of our finest vegetables came from seeds which he bred with love and energy rather than chemicals.

Intellectual—Yellow

1. Seed meditation. How does a tiny seed grow into a flower? A tree? How can an egg become a bird with colorful feathers? A rooster? An insect? A fish? A human? Follow the growth process from seed to tree, from egg to bird. Image all the details. Ask questions. Consider different answers. Discuss it as a wonder of nature. Science intellectually understands the process but no man can duplicate what nature has done. No man can even make a blade of grass.

2. The intellect lives in a world of questions and answers. Take a thought, any thought. Call it a "seed thought" and make it grow. See what that thought leads to, what ideas it brings. Take a crazy thought, then a serious thought. For example, take the thought of a wriggling snake . . . what comes into your mind? Yick, brown, slimy, smooth, scary, lives in caves, creepy, bites, charm, Eve, poison, colorful, diamond pattern, ugly, beautiful, trying to get out of something . . . and so on. Everyone join in.

3. How good are we with details? Pair off and each person have a pen and two sheets of paper. Each person draw a simple picture, a symbol, an object, a tree, etc. Don't show the other person. Then, one at a time, describe your drawing in detail to the other and see if the other can copy it exactly just by your description. Tell him where to put a line and where to put a dot, and so forth. Then when you have both finished drawing each other's drawing compare the results. How did you do? Pair off with different partners and see who gives the best instructions and who does the best listening and transcribing.

4. After doing a meditation ask yourself Who am I? For three minutes write down all the answers that come to your Being as to "Who am I?" or tell them to someone else.

5.   Science experiments. As a family, discover together and experiment with how a car battery works, how a three-way light bulb works to bring in more energy, how a walkie-talkie, a radio, TV, tape recorder, etc., work. Relate all these appliances to energy and discuss how energy works similarly in humans when we recharge, when we meditate and when we can do telepathy or project images. Explore the science of energy together using library books, science kits or games, and your own creative thinking.

Social—Orange

In this level we work with our social conditioning and our relationships with others.

1.   This exercise has been called the Full Length Mirror because we are looking at ourselves, full length, in each other. Each person acts as a mirror to reflect what he sees in the person in front of him that is good. Here every statement must be positive, nothing critical. We want to build positive self-images to develop true potential. Whatever comes to you that is positive about the other, say it. Be real and true to yourself. Don't worry about what the other will think. Line up: one person faces the line, and begins by telling the first person in the line what he sees or experiences. Take about one minute with each person. Then the next person takes a turn being the mirror and goes down the line. Repeat until everyone has been the mirror.

2.   Getting into other's worlds. Someone act as leader and think of a place in town that everyone in the group knows. It can be a park, a building, a restaurant, a tree anywhere. In turn each person describes that place from a different viewpoint taken from the following list or one that the leader makes up: a dog, a bird in the sky, a tree, an ant, a three-year-old girl, a six-year old boy, a ten-year-old boy, a thirteen-year-old girl, a lady in a wheelchair, a busy mother, a father.

3. Honesty exercises. The following exercises are called honesty exercises because to do them properly we have to be really honest with the others. This means not hiding our feelings because we are afraid we might cause problems or hurt others by talking about something we don't like in them. We will actually help them more if we can share our deepest and most honest feelings in a selfless way. Then we have the opportunity to get in touch with what it is that disturbs us in another. By bringing it out we can work on it. Just rationalizing it away or arguing it away inside often represses it and doesn't help. It's the things that disturb us that are valuable teachers to learn from. For if we changed our minds we wouldn't be disturbed. It's what disturbs us— the fears, jealousies, resentments and doubts in ourselves and in our family that we need to work on to perfect our lives.

In all these honesty exercises we must remember that real listening means getting beyond our own thoughts that surface or come to mind as another is talking. We must give our whole attention to really receive the other. If we start talking about something off the subject, we are not really listening. It means we are being self-centered, caught up in our own ideas and thoughts and not into the being of the other.

a. Mirroring. After having meditated (the meditation on p. 111 is especially good to begin this session), two people pair off and sit knee to knee facing each other. The others observe them as they practice mirroring. First one, then the other tells as nitty-gritty as he can how he feels about himself right now and how he feels about his relationship with the other. The other in the pair listens, with his mind empty, like a photographic plate receiving the words and the feelings and thoughts behind them. He practices true conscious identification with the other, really opening to receive and become one with the other person. Then, when the first person is done, the second person mirrors the first person back as he knows him to be, as he is experiencing him to be. He mirrors back the words and then he mirrors back what he feels is the real meaning behind the words. If he is unsure about anything he can ask the first person a question to clear it up. The idea is to really become the other so that he can see himself come back. The others watch and make notes as to what is true mirroring and what is poor listening, what is a projection or a basic assumption coming from the person who is mirroring. (See the Glossary on page 150 to better understand these terms.) When the second person has finished mirroring, the others give him the feedback as to what they saw. Then the pair switches roles and repeats the exercise. The group rotates with a new pair in the middle.

It is amazing how poor most of us listen. This fact will come out in the exercise. We hear the words but not the real meaning, or we twist up the words to suit our own understanding or we start talking about something off the subject. This exercise is very important for clearing our filter mirrors, and with practice will enable us to penetrate beneath them in ourself and others. It will draw us much closer to our loved ones with whom we do it. If there are only two people and no watchers available, use a tape recorder and play it back to discover the projections, basic assumptions and listening problems.

b.   Sit in a circle and have each member of the family say, in a few sentences, as deeply as they can, what they feel each of the others thinks about them and how they think about themselves. Is it the same? Don't get into a discussion, just go around. If you have a tape recorder record the exercise. When you are finished going around you can add comments and insights. Try to get into what are the projections or basic assumptions. Then repeat the exercise, going deeper into your feelings the second time. Wait a day or two and then listen to the tape recorder playback. Note how much more you hear in it.

c.   Say one thing to each family member that you've wanted to say to them and never have (usually we let a great deal pass which builds up inside about the other, never really feeling we have the right, safe opportunity to say it, or dismissing it as not really important). Now is the time to say what we feel. Go around and take turns.

    d.   Love seat. One person sits in the middle of the circle and faces each of the others in turn. The others, one by one, say one positive thing they really like about the person and one thing they feel the person needs to improve or work on. No two people may say the same thing. Someone is the recorder and makes a chart like a grid of what is said and who said it. Each person also makes statements about himself, so all the squares on the chart are filled. (See page 54 for more explanation.)

    4.   Squabble time. When there is a family squabble, or a conflict between any two members of the family we can call "Squabble Time," and go into one of the following exercises which will help to make the conflict creative and growth-producing. Usually the biggest problem in "squabbles" is that someone is not really listening to the other. Either the child or adult doesn't feel their viewpoint is really getting across or understood.

In dealing with squabbles we have to become Centered first. Then we have to become honest with ourself about what we are really feeling. Only then can we be honest with others or be able to get quiet enough to really listen to others. Sometimes we may realize we are taking out some built-up frustration about a job on a family member. The best thing might be for us to cool off for awhile by taking a shower or by beating a pillow with a bat, or running around the block a couple of times. When we are ready to interact we begin with the mirroring exercise as given on p.141. We center, will our emotions and thoughts to calm, and tune into the One. Then we tell the other where we are really at and they listen and mirror back what we've said until we are satisfied that they have heard us and understood what we meant. Then the other person has a turn and tells us where they're at and we listen and mirror back until they're satisfied that we've heard and understood. With a little practice of this exercise we will soon learn how to mirror even under stressful situations. We make sure we are really communicating instead of just answering back when someone speaks out at us. This way we avoid negative arguments. Instead we may say, "I hear you saying you want more freedom. Does this mean you are feeling hemmed in at our home?" And so on. Find out where each person is really at.

Still, it is often difficult to really see, hear and experience from another person's point of view, especially when emotions keep stirring. To help us learn how we can get into another's world better we can do a simple role-switching exercise. In role switching we use two chairs and one person. If son Phil is having a problem with Dad, Phil will sit in one chair and pretend Dad is in the empty chair. (The real Dad doesn't speak.) Phil will talk to Dad in the "empty" chair and tell him how he feels. Then Phil will switch roles and sit in the other chair. He will become Dad and will answer to Phil in the first chair, telling Phil how he feels. Then Phil will switch back to the first chair and be himself again talking to "Dad" in the empty chair. Each time he switches he tries to really identify and get inside Dad's or his own world. He keeps the exercise going until he feels he has gone as far as he can. If someone else in the family feels there is more to go into they can ask Phil to continue and prod him with a few questions. This exercise is excellent for anyone— husband, wife or children as young as four or five. For those eager to go deeper we can do some simple psychodrama. We take a real problem scene from life, like the latest unresolved family argument or some situation that is bothering someone. The person with the problem plays himself, but everyone else switches roles. For example, if Mother has a big argument with twelve-year-old daughter Jane then Mother acts herself in the scene and nine-year-old daughter Karen or fifteen-year-old son Tom plays how Jane feels as best they can. Jane and the others watch. When one of the watchers has an insight into something deeper that Mother or the person playing Jane is really feeling they stand behind one of them and play that part along with them, like a double. They say the deeper thing they really feel is going on.

Another role-switching psychodrama is for the whole family to play different roles and take turns acting each other out in nitty-gritty situations so we get to see how everyone else in our family experiences us. When it is over we share how we felt about each other. What surprised us? What seemed right on? What seemed way off? How do others see it?

Physical—Red

1. Lifting exercise.

One person sits in a chair. Four people stand around him. With just the forefingers they try to pick up the person. One person puts his forefingers under one shoulder, one person puts his forefingers under the other shoulder, one person puts his forefingers under one knee and the fourth person puts his forefingers under the other knee. All lift . . . Does the person come off the chair? Then everyone piles their hands in layers above the head of the one in the chair, but they make sure not to touch hands. They all draw energy into the hands, feeling the energy come in and soak it up. Then, at the count of 1, 2, 3, quickly everyone moves to lift the person in the same way as before. 1, 2, 3, change— presto— it's easy.

2. Roughhouse

Everyone stands alone in the room and feels his or her own body. Start with the head and move down to the toes, rubbing and patting every bit of your body. Then have a free-for-all tumbling game, being careful not to hurt sensitive little people or even sensitive big people. Frolic and giggle, tickle and hug. Massage each other's backs and touch faces. Do it all with love.

3. Five Senses

a. Touch exercise. For every blindfolded person one person should not be blindfolded. Lead the blindfolded person around outdoors, barefoot. Lead them to touch different parts of nature— mud, grass, the bark of a tree, a velvety flower petal, etc. Be sure to watch that they don't step on anything sharp or trip over anything. This is also a trust exercise and the sighted person should feel responsible for the well-being of the blindfolded person.

b. Taste exercise. Still blindfolded, have the person taste different spices and different foods to try to identify them.

c. Smell exercise. Again, still blindfolded lead the person around the house and have him describe all the different smells you lead him to. Or, if it is easier, bring different smells to the person and have him identify them.

d. Sound exercise. Still blindfolded, say all the different sounds you can hear over a five-minute period to someone else who writes them down. Do it far enough from others who are doing the same exercise.

e. Sight exercise. Take off the blindfold and look around at the room you are in. Try to take in every detail. Go into another room and write down everything you can remember that was in that room, every detail. Or, if you are too little to write, tell everything you can remember to someone else who writes it down for you.

4. Food awareness.

Have a meal together where each person feeds the other. No knives, spoons or forks can be used, only fingers. Everyone, from baby to adult, feeds each other. Get close enough together to minimize slopping, or have it outside as a picnic.

5. Movement to music.

Turn on some music and everyone dance, hop, fly, spring, whatever— just move to the music. Join with a partner, change partners, or go it alone, however you feel. Include different kinds of music, rock, blues, jazz, classical, etc.

6. Arts and crafts.

Any kind of artistic expression is a good creative outlet for our energies. Energies taken in during meditation need creative expression to be properly eliminated, just like we need to eliminate food we eat after it is digested. Arts and crafts help us to ground the energy right down to earth and bring different levels together like the imaginative and the physical. Family art activities are great fun. For example, try spreading a large sheet of wrapping paper or newsprint and do a family group painting or a family collage. Meditate first, and try to keep tuned into Center as you create, making your creation a meditation in action.

Center Symbol of Nuclear Evolution. Copyright 1959 Christopher Hills

Afterword

Having traveled this far together we now have a good insight into what needs to be done to bring about the deeper love and contact with our children that most parents crave. We have provided the ingredients and the recipe for a true nuclear family. Now the next step is to make the cake by repeatedly practicing all of the meditations and exercises, experiencing their fruits and creating new variations of our own. When the cake is properly baked in this way, it will be a treat fit for the gods to eat.

Those of us who are eager to provide our children with the best possible opportunity for a rich and fulfilling life and who genuinely want the evolution that is offered in this book will certainly do the practice.

DEBORAH ROZMAN

Deborah Rozman, Ph.D., is also the author of *Meditating With Children: The Art of Concentration and Centering* and co-author of *Exploring Inner Space: Awareness Games for All Ages* (University of the Trees Press) – new consciousness books for parents, teachers and teenagers. She has studied psychology and the nature of consciousness for many years. Ms. Rozman has been Director of the Psychology of Consciousness program at University of the Trees. She attended University of Chicago, University of California at Santa Cruz and University of the Trees. Ms. Rozman is an educational consultant and has done workshops and in-service training programs for many public and private schools throughout the country. She has taught transpersonal psychology, creative communication, centering, visualization and meditation to all age groups in California Public Schools. Her books have been sponsored by superintendents of several school districts and by church leaders as effective learning tools.

Since 1987 Ms. Rozman has embarked on a new journey into even more rewarding and evolving dimensions of life as described in Chapter 0.

BRIEF GLOSSARY OF
UNUSUAL WORDS USED IN TEXT

Aura—The radiance around the body which is of different colors depending on our level of consciousness. It can be seen by learning how to readjust our vision to subtler frequencies of light.

Centering—Contacting the inner center of being, the nucleus or soul. When we center, we gather our energies together and become calm.

Creative Imagination—The level of consciousness which uses the creative energies of consciousness to recreate its experience by combining will and imagination and projecting the image into life.

Ego—The self-sense that feels we are separate from other selves, from space. The self that says you are outside over there and I am over here inside my body.

Evolution—The growth of intelligence that awakens life and consciousness to its full potential.

Filters—The personality layers built from birth that block direct perception and block the clear light from manifesting purely through us.

Karma—Cause and Effect. Newton's law of every action has an equal and opposite reaction applied to human actions and thoughts. It is the chain of thought and actions which determine our future thoughts and actions and their consequences.

Kundalini—The creative force of consciousness which is aroused when the male and female energies in the spinal channels are exactly balanced.

Mandala—A visual aid to non-conceptual thinking. It takes us beyond the normal mental process and can be used successfully only after the mind is concentrated.

Mantra—A silent or verbal word that is used in prayer or meditation to help quiet the mind. It is also used to protect us against wrong thinking. The word mantra means *mind power* in Sanskrit.

Meditation—The practice of direct perception of wisdom.

Mirroring—Seeing ourself reflected in the world and being able to reflect back accurately what someone says to us, both their words and their real meaning.

Self—ego or personality. Identifying with our personality.

Self, Real Self, True Self—Going into the Source at the Center within we realize we are not only our bodies but that there is an essence beyond personality which includes all others in it Self.

Source—The center within that radiates all consciousness. Can be seen and experienced as a central sun inside during meditation.

Toning—Sounding primal sounds like Ahhh or Oooommm and mantras to create rich vibrations and resonances. These resonances still the mind.

BOOKS, TAPES AND GAMES FOR HEALTHY FAMILIES...

NEW !
The Crystal Lady,
by Deborah Rozman
(ages 5 and up)
Deborah Rozman introduces children to the magical world of the heart in this enchanting story book, exquisitely illustrated by Sandy Royall. Cherie and Davey go on an adventure to their "heart crystal" and find out how to stay in their heart. They learn the tools that any child can relate to for transforming bad days into good ones and discovering that life really is a gift. At the end of the book the Crystal Lady gives them and the reader a beautiful, valuable surprise gift.
Hardcover Book with gift: $19.95

Fluffy and Sparky: A Story about True Buddies,
by Paula Elliott
(for ages 3 and up)
Fluffy and Sparky is the delightful story of two little sea otters who each become tired of playing all alone. Their adventures together teach children about the fun that comes from sharing their playfulness, and their love with a buddy. Illustrated by Sandy Royall.
Hardcover Book: $12.95

Buddy Bubbles: Games for a Child's Heart,
by Deborah Rozman
(for ages 2 to 6)
The poetry and music on this tape guide young children into their deeper heart. They learn the difference between being in their heart and happy and being out of their heart and fussy, angry or upset. They discover that their soft heart is their very best buddy, who they can talk to anytime and get real, helpful answers. They learn that their own heart is a magical gift and lots of fun!
cassette tape: $8.95

The Heart Way,
by Deborah Rozman
(for ages 6 to 12)
Many older children and adults will love *The Heart Way,* and enjoy the experience of discovering their own heart power. All magic in life comes from the heart, where we can learn how to find a deeper and better feeling whenever we want to. From the heart, life looks different, problems resolve much more quickly, intuition and imagination are sparked and love flows easily. Poetry and music accompany fun games and narration for a relaxed experience rich in texture, imagination and heartfelt fun.
cassette tape: $8.95

Heart Zones, *by Lew Childre*
(for all ages)
This beautiful music tape was specifically designed to release stress and promote positive moods in children and adults. Biofeedback tests show that listening to *Heart Zones* helps you relax and feel good about yourself, through beautiful melodies, unusual rhythmic effects and upbeat tempo. Experiments show that repeated listening to *Heart Zones* has proven effective for:
*enhancing creativity and learning ability,
*creating closer communication
*promoting restful sleep before bedtime
*slowing down and enhancing manageability in children by creating a more receptive state of listening from the heart.
cassette tape: $9.95

Heart Treasure Chest and Game
(for all ages)
A delightful, fun game that you can play alone or with friends and family to help put you on your highest and happiest path in life. Each of the 27 cards has a different message to bring growth, happiness and a deeper understanding of life. Guaranteed to bring you and your family or friends closer together and transform negative moods and feelings into positive ones. This card game comes packaged in a treasure chest full of fun tools along with the *Heart Zones* music tape to help you find your deeper heart intuition in the daily game of life. Instead of walking the plank, find the buried treasure inside your heart.
Set of 27 cards, game booklet, tools, and Heart Zones cassette tape : $19.95

More Books and Tapes For Healthy Families...

Meditating With Children: The Art of Concentration and Centering,
by Deborah Rozman
Meditating With Children is considered by many educational authorities to be the finest book ever written on the value of meditation exercises for children to enhance calmness, creativity and listening skills. Children of all ages love its fun, simple techniques, which are in use in many public and private schools (pre-school through high school). This book is especially stimulating for teenagers who wish to develop their concentration and imagination and build their self-esteem.   *Book:* $10.95

Cassette tape of meditations from the book by Deborah Rozman $9.95

Joy in the Classroom,
by Stephanie Herzog
At a time when our educational systems are in crisis, Stephanie Herzog's straight-from-the-heart reflections on her 13 pioneering years in public school classrooms are a breath of fresh air. As she learns to awaken children to their deeper selves using communication skills, centering and visualization, they discover their own inner wisdom and ability to transform their relationships and emotional life. Describes how to implement centering activities within a school.   *Book:* $6.95

The Ultimate Kid: Levels of Learning that Make a Differen
by Jeffrey Goelitz
Jeffrey Goelitz gives 44 lesson plans w games and creative play designed to inject fun into learning and growing a stimulate all levels of a child's being, including the sensory, social, intellectual, emotional, conceptual, intuitive and imaginative. This book helps children create a balanced understanding of who they are and ho they relate to the world.   *Book:* $8.95

Communing With the Spirit of Your Unborn Child,
by Dawson Church
This "excellent" book, "an outstanding addition to prenatal literature" (*Midwifery Today*) is a clear how-to manual for parents exploring pregnan birth and infancy from a spiritual perspective. Using photographs, diagrams and meditations, this powe classic outlines in simple, practical language a step-by-step approach that enables parents to communicate wih inner magic of their unborn child.
  Book: $8.95, *audio tape:* $9.95

Aslan Publishing
Planetary Publications
14795 West Park Ave.
Boulder Creek, CA 95006

1-800-372-3100

Please call us to place an order o put your name on our mailing lis receive information on new upcoming books, games and tap

Quantity Discounts!

Buy 2 items, get $2 off
Buy 3 items, get $3 off
Buy 4 items, get $4 off, etc.
Order Now!